THESE SIGNS WILL ACCOMPANY THOSE WHO BELIEVE: IN MY NAME THEY WILL DRIVE OUT DEMONS.
—MARK 16:17

how to cast out demons

A GUIDE TO THE BASICS

DORIS M. WAGNER

A Division of Gospel Light
Ventura, California, U.S.A.

Published by Renew Books
From Gospel Light
Ventura, California, U.S.A.
Printed in the U.S.A.

Renew Books is a ministry of Gospel Light, an evangelical Christian publisher dedicated to serving the local church. We believe God's vision for Gospel Light is to provide church leaders with biblical, user-friendly materials that will help them evangelize, disciple and minister to children, youth and families.

It is our prayer that this Renew book will help you discover biblical truth for your own life and help you meet the needs of others. May God richly bless you.

For a free catalog of resources from Renew Books/Gospel Light please call your Christian supplier or contact us at 1-800-4-GOSPEL *or* www.regalbooks.com.

How to Cast Out Demons: A Guide to the Basics was originally published by Wagner Institute for Practical Ministry in 1999.

Cover Design by Kevin Keller
Interior Design by Rob Williams

LIBRARY OF CONGRESS CATALOGING-IN-PUBLICATION DATA
Wagner, Doris M., 1932-
How to cast out demons : a guide to the basics / Doris Wagner.
p. cm.
ISBN 0-8307-2535-0 (trade paper)
1. Exorcism–Handbooks, manuals, etc. I. Title.

BV873.E8 W34 2000
265′.94–dc21 99-056254

2 3 4 5 6 7 8 9 10 11 12 13 14 15 / 09 08 07 06 05 04 03 02

Rights for publishing this book in other languages are contracted by Gospel Light Worldwide, the international nonprofit ministry of Gospel Light. Gospel Light Worldwide also provides publishing and technical assistance to international publishers dedicated to producing Sunday School and Vacation Bible School curricula and books in the languages of the world. For additional information, visit www.gospellightworldwide.org; write to Gospel Light Worldwide, P.O. Box 3875, Ventura, CA 93006; or send an e-mail to info@gospellightworldwide.org.

contents

SECTION 3
the questionnaire as an effective tool

appendices

INTRODUCTION

how i got involved

How in the world did a little old grandma ever get involved in such yucky stuff? My story so strongly resembles most of the others I have heard or read about that it makes me smile. I never went looking for a deliverance ministry—it found me.

I stand amazed at what God has done in my life to prepare me for this ministry that began almost 20 years ago. I was already a mature person, my missionary service behind me, and I was now in a position to help train younger missionaries to do a better job than I did. I considered myself a young, enthusiastic worker who went to the mission field with a handicap: inadequate training for the job that awaited me.

My husband, Peter, and I were all heart, but we had been poorly prepared for overseas service. Excellent theologians, Bible teachers, Christian educators, preachers and personal evangelists had taught us, but not missionaries. We knew next to nothing about the cross-cultural communication of the gospel, because the field of missiology had not yet been developed in the early 1950s. Courses in anthropology, language and cultural learning, as well as specialized teaching in Islam, Hinduism, Buddhism, animism and folk religions were not available in our schools. The cessationist theology of our training left no room for praying for the sick or casting out demons, and it was the only theology that we knew.

We did all sorts of missionary work in Bolivia during the ensuing 16 years, but we mainly worked in evangelism, theological education and mission administration. Shortly after we had moved out of the small town of San José to Bolivia's second largest city of Cochabamba, Peter became the general director of the Andes Evangelical Mission and I became the office manager of the same mission.

Peter had been either a student or a teacher most of his life, so during the times when he was not teaching he became a student and continued working on degrees. One of the study times that turned our world upside down and changed the course of our lives was when Peter was studying a Master of Arts in Missiology from his alma mater, Fuller Theological Seminary. Peter had been reading Donald McGavran's writings to investigate the field of missiology more closely; and it was during this study time, from 1967 to 1968, that things finally fell into place and the term "power encounter" became part of our vocabulary.

We were beginning to tap into a whole new realm of possibility for missionary work!

Peter and I have always had the somewhat dubious reputation of being about 10 years ahead of the pack as far as a comfort zone is concerned. If we feel it's God's will, new ground is never a threat to us. It has worried our colleagues at times, and it has made our evangelical crowd embarrassed about us now and then. But we just had to know more about this "power" stuff.

getting in touch with power encounter

Anthropologist Alan Tippett, a missionary from Australia to Fiji, was the first to teach this new concept to us. In simple terms, a power encounter is a situation created by presenting the gospel to some unreached people group that precipitates a showdown of sorts as to who is the more powerful: the pagan god of the group or Jehovah God and His Son, Jesus Christ. When Jehovah God won the encounter—and that is what the class taught the students how to present—a "people movement" would often occur. This meant that people would become Christians in groups, often burning fetishes or making other public statements of their faith in Christ. It was new teaching and we liked it! However, it put the missionaries on the spot because they then had to know how to handle this "power."

We were game to learn. We wanted to become more effective in winning the lost in larger numbers, but it smacked a little of the Pentecostal/charismatic territory with which we were unfamiliar. We knew it was right and that we believed it, but implementing and teaching it were still a few steps away.

Peter was invited to remain at the Fuller Seminary School of World Mission as a professor when his degree was complete, but we were not ready to leave Bolivia yet. So we returned for another three years to get things on solid footing there and moved back to California in 1971 to start life all over again. Peter had arranged with the administration that if he were hired, we came as a pair and I would be his secretary. This was considered by some a little odd; and there was actually a rule, somewhere on the books, which stated that husband and wife could not work together, but Peter was insistent—I was part of the package. They gave in and we have worked together ever since. He became associate professor of Church Growth and Latin American Studies. I served as his secretary, worked with the publicity committee and was the oversight of all technical aspects of dissertations and theses.

Church growth was our specialty, both here and abroad. Our personalized California license plates were MT 28 19 and MT 28 20—the Great Commission. We got to know many pastors of growing churches, first as students and then as examples for Peter's other students as they studied their churches and wrote papers on church-growth principles they had learned in class.

JOHN WIMBER SHOWS UP

One of these bright students, John Wimber, appeared one day to take a class. He was your typical Quaker pastor, except that he was a rather recent convert who had come out of the music business. His skills were music and management before his conversion. He soon became a personal evangelist like few we have known. His church grew dramatically and he wanted to help other churches grow. We became good friends with John and Carol. Eventually Peter asked John to help him teach church growth, so he resigned from his church and came to work for us. The way opened up for him to consult with churches and denominations as well. But with his tremendous gift of evangelism, he soon grew disquieted in his spirit and asked if he could start a church on the side—sort of moonlighting. And that is how the Vineyard Christian Fellowship got its humble beginning. John had to leave us to devote his full time to the Vineyard, but we remained good friends and we often visited the Vineyard on Sunday evenings. It's where the action was in the Los Angeles area at the time!

The Lord led John into praying for the sick. He recounts how it was in sheer obedience, without much result for a number of months. Then it happened—their first divine healing took place, one of hundreds, if not thousands more that followed. Peter invited John to teach a class on praying for the sick at Fuller, and we jumped in also. Many were healed, and we were having the time of our lives. This met with some opposition among certain of our colleagues, but we pressed forward knowing that God wanted us to teach our students to be better missionaries than we were.

Now, here comes the connection you've been waiting for. You don't pray for the sick very long before emotional disturbances pop up and a demon manifests with loud screams and bodily contortions. That's how I encountered my first demon. I didn't look for it; it came to me and I had to do something about it.

Since this power stuff had moved closer to home, I wanted to learn all I could about it, so I attended a class on the theory of demonology that Carol Wimber was teaching at the Anaheim Vineyard. Those four hours of teaching qualified me to be the family expert on demons. It was right after that when our first demon introduced itself.

FACE-TO-FACE WITH THE FIRST DEMON!

A young woman heard that Peter was especially successful in praying for bad backs and skeletal disorders. She was a Fuller student, so she made an appointment for Peter to pray for her in our office area. As Peter approached her forehead with some anointing oil, the demon manifested and screams erupted. I immediately approached her and said, "Stop it!" Her body froze and there was a dead silence. I commanded the demon to give its name, and a masculine voice slowly and deliberately hissed, "Lust."

Peter was impressed. He grabbed his legal pad and a pencil and stood back, taking notes furiously. I took over and did the best I could, commanding the demon to leave. As others manifested, I took authority over them and told them to go also in the name of Jesus. My guess is that Fuller had neither heard nor seen such boisterous excitement coming out of a professor's office in some time!

IF WE DO IT, LET'S DO IT WELL

I was determined to better learn how to do this. I began to seek out books on the subject of casting out demons and little by little learned and became adept at it. I encountered an elderly couple in Australia named Noel and Phyl Gibson. They had produced some excellent books and workbooks and, God bless them, they took me under their wings and apprenticed me from afar. When I had an especially tough case, I would fax them and they would respond immediately. They were the best friends I ever had whom I had never met!

I soon had more people requesting deliverance than I had time for. It takes me two to three hours to adequately pray for a person, and I can pray for them only once because I am currently CEO of a multimillion-dollar ministry that is very demanding. That ministry is Global Harvest Ministries and the World Prayer Center here in Colorado Springs. I must now limit my praying to Christian workers only, but I teach all I can so that more and more people are trained in deliverance.

My dream is to see hundreds and eventually thousands of churches with an effective deliverance ministry all around the world. When Jesus said, "Freely you have received, freely give" (Matt. 10:8), He was referring to healing the sick and casting out demons. The second part of that dream is to see churches with qualified staff professionals who operate as deliverance ministers.

I realize more than ever how God prepared me from "ages ago" to do and eventually teach deliverance. He honored the fact that I believed every word of the Bible. As I tried to live it out, He gave me the faith to believe that, indeed, Jesus is the same, yesterday, today and forever. He gave me loving and compassionate parents and a husband who was the same so that I could reflect that to needy people.

My personality type is that of a phlegmatic, a peacemaker who can't stand conflict. I asked the Lord why He put me in the position of having to deal with demons when I like peace around me. Then it dawned on me that my job was to fix it so others could have the peace from torment for which they long. So, I am a "fix-it" person. My prayer is that this practical book will help those of you called to this ministry to take advantage of what it has taken me years to learn.

FINALLY, BE STRONG IN THE LORD AND IN HIS MIGHTY POWER. PUT ON THE FULL ARMOR OF GOD SO THAT YOU CAN TAKE YOUR STAND AGAINST THE DEVIL'S SCHEMES.
—EPHESIANS 6:10,11 (NIV)

SECTION 1

the basics for spiritual deliverance

CHAPTER 1

demythologizing demonology

Many folk come to my seminars, called "Understanding Basic Issues in Deliverance," with a bit of fear and trepidation. Some are filled with a sort of bold timidity, wanting to learn but still wondering what they've let themselves in for. They become much more at ease when I show up, because of my appearance: elderly, plump and short. Although I'm not very gray at all, I struggle to make it on stage with my walker and in my tennis shoes, with a brace on one foot, and a heavy limp due to one artificial knee and two artificial hips that weren't totally successful implants. They can tell that I hurt in my joints due to a case of arthritis, and I need to lecture from a seated position because of my inability to stand for more than a few minutes at a time. I really look pretty harmless, if not even a tad helpless! To people I may look harmless and a little handicapped, but to demons I am a formidable foe due to years of experience in the ministry of deliverance. Since I am now training others to minister deliverance, I suppose the kingdom of darkness is even more unhappy.

what is deliverance?

The Random House Dictionary of the English Language (New York, NY: Random House, 1967), unabridged, has an excellent definition for deliverance. Although certainly not theologically slanted, the dictionary gives a very accurate definition. Definition #7 for "deliver" reads, "To set free or liberate: *They were delivered from bondage.*" Two synonyms for definition #7 are "emancipate" and "release." In this book, we will be using the word with this exact definition in mind. The fact that the italicized phrase "They were delivered from bondage" was used gave this definition a perfect meaning for our purposes.

Much of a general ministry of deliverance can be learned. I would even say that it could be an acquired skill, and that with experience and the help of the Holy Spirit, it can become a valuable ministry tool. Some seem more gifted than others, but it is hard to get away from the fact that Jesus told His followers to do it. So every Christian should have the basic ability to cast out a demon. Even the disciples got to see Jesus do it and to apprentice with Him for a few years. They got to ask Him questions after their first evangelistic trip; and when they asked, "Why could we not cast it out?" (Mark 9:28) they were instructed that there are different kinds of demons and that "This kind can come out by nothing but prayer and fasting" (Mark 9:29). So instruction is helpful along the way. My prayer is that this basic manual will help many of you receive a burden for those in bondage and that you will go and set the captives free.

SOME MISUNDERSTANDINGS

In the past there have been some misunderstandings about casting out demons. I have heard of several deaths because of mistreatment when demons were manifesting, such as holding a person down and placing pressure on an artery until a heart attack ensued. Another couple tried to bludgeon a demon out of their son with a cement block and he died of injuries. A grandmother in New York fed her five-year-old granddaughter a lethal mixture of ammonia, vinegar, cayenne pepper and olive oil because the child's relatives thought she was full of the devil. She died of course. I have these cases documented but will spare you further details. Casting out demons has gained a bad reputation in some circles because of misunderstanding and abuse.

I believe the most unfortunate reason why people have misgivings about deliverance is that they were prayed over once and "it didn't work." People are often far too hasty in casting out a demon without knowing why it is there and dealing with that entry point. They scream at a demon of rejection or lust, but, in an attempt to cure the symptom, they neglect the cause. The person may have temporary relief, but before long, if the entry point has not been healed, the demon returns again and may bring along more demons. The unfortunate problem is that there are too many good-hearted people out there who have never learned how to minister to the whole personality of an individual.

Another misunderstanding arises from the fact that we are dealing with the invisible world and can't see with our eyes what is going on. It has taken on a "spooky" aura. People don't like to mess with something they don't understand well or that they can't even see. Some of my friends have an unusually keen sense of discernment and can literally see demonic beings. They are usually correct, but I don't have a strong gift of discernment at all. However, my "gift of deduction" is rather advanced. Once you've been in this business for any length of time, things fall into very predictable patterns, and I am convinced that a great deal of the ministry of casting out demons can be learned.

It is with a bit of tongue in cheek that I let you in on some observations and slight accusations leveled toward me and a deliverance ministry when I was just starting out.

Accuser: You are using the name of Jesus as though it were Christian magic. We need to be careful about that.
Granny: I'd sure hate to face a demon without it.

Accuser: I don't believe in demons.
Granny: Wanna follow me around for a week?

Accuser: You see a demon behind every bush.
Granny: Not so, but if there is one behind a bush, I want to make sure it leaves.

Accuser: But the sign gifts went out with the Early Church.
Granny: I choose to believe they did not, and operate from that paradigm. The fat file of testimonies I have from grateful people who have found freedom cause me to believe otherwise. I like to think that Jesus' teachings are for today. Life has been much more exciting and fulfilling for me since I learned that "faith is fun." And Jesus just doesn't let me down!

Accuser: Why is the way you cast out demons so long and arduous? Didn't Jesus cast them out with just a couple of words?
Granny: Since I'm not the second person of the Trinity, I just have to do the best I can. I've tried to do shortcuts,

but the longer way seems more thorough. I can pray for a person only once, so I need to do my best with those couple of hours.

We just can't escape Jesus' mandate to "heal the sick, cleanse the lepers, raise the dead, cast out demons" (Matt. 10:8). I was a member of a panel that dealt with power ministries recently and, when the moderator of the panel was unable to come at the last minute, I sat down and quickly slapped together a 10-minute segment that was assigned to me. I selected the topic of "The Need for Deliverance Ministry Today." I was so amazed at the message God gave me for a 10-minute talk that I would like to share it with you here. It had two parts: Our Disadvantaged Society and Our Disadvantaged Church.

The Church today needs more and better equipment to minister to society because of grave circumstances and problems that have arisen in the latter half of this century. Much of the basic teaching of the Christian faith is being challenged openly. Several things came to my mind immediately as I took pen in hand.

our disadvantaged society

1. *The Fatherlessness of This Generation*
   Extremely high divorce rates have torn homes apart and moms have to work and struggle to make ends meet. Kids are often alone and have TV for their teacher. Instability, insecurity and uncertainty are a part of life. Many kids can't understand the concept of a loving heavenly Father because they have never seen a loving earthly father. Common demonic entry points

can include rejection, unforgiveness, abandonment and many others.

2. *Tolerance Triumphs over Truth*
   This is excessive tolerance. Whether it is right or not, the worst thing one can do nowadays is to be intolerant. This has been a factor in advancing the homosexual agenda. People are all mixed up because they are taught that tolerance is *always* appropriate. Faith is challenged and Christians are snubbed because they are intolerant. The Bible gives us rules of faith and practice, but it is becoming wrong out there to talk about them.

3. *Political Correctness*
   PC behavior is also stressed as a virtue, no matter what is correct morally, socially or biblically. The homosexual community has had free reign in pushing their agenda into schools, the workplace and government. Since it is talked about so much, it is being practiced more, and vicious sexual demons are taking advantage of easy openings.

4. *The Acceptance of Permissiveness*
   It's okay to do almost anything. As a result, experimentation opens doors to demons of lust, addiction, violence and other such things.

5. *Lack of Teaching Regarding Morals on Right and Wrong*
   When I was growing up, my little one-room country schoolhouse did not have the Ten Commandments on the wall, but to cheat, steal, lie, swear or be disrespectful

was not tolerated. In those days, a child could be punished with a ruler and a note was sent home to the parents. It seemed to me that the kids who were taught high standards at home pitched in to teach the more disadvantaged. Kids are more comfortable knowing what their parameters are. Some are adrift today because they have no course charted for them. It is easy to do wrong when you don't know right from wrong.

6. *The Negative Influences of Things Such as Movies, TV and Certain Music*
   With so much violence, skewed values and improper sexual input bombarding the minds and eyes of society, it is no wonder that after a time Generation X has become callused and confused and they just don't know right from wrong. But worse yet, they have almost no concept of evil, as I recently read in *Leadership* journal. This is very scary. It leaves them vulnerable to innocently inviting demons into their lives because they just don't know any better.

7. *Rejection of Biblical Values*
   Even if they are taught well at home, parents still struggle with their kids at times because "it's just not cool" to have biblical values. Peer pressure can get through to some. It is becoming increasingly necessary to teach our youngsters to swim upstream, against the current. Absolutes are biblical, but society today wants relativism.

   I believe the general consensus is that it is more difficult to raise a family today than it was some time ago, and this, coupled with open invitations to the demonic, requires a Church that is well equipped to help in this area. Unfortunately, as I pointed out in the second section of my 10-minute speech, in many cases the Church is not prepared.

our disadvantaged church

1. *Cessationism*

   The teaching of the doctrine of cessationism has led much of the Church into disbelief in the supernatural, including miracles, praying for the sick and casting out demons. This doctrine states that these "sign gifts" died off with the apostolic age and that there is no need for them today because we now have the written Word of God, which is all we need for faith and practice. This has opened the door to holy disbelief that doesn't encourage faith in these things. It has made a large segment of the Church disadvantaged. Fortunately, however, cessationism is rapidly losing its popularity.

2. *Poor Teaching*

   The Church is really short on biblical teaching. I'm not sure to what this can be attributed, but I do know that today many rebel at being told that there are such things as rules. You have to go a long way to find a large congregation well versed in general Bible content, the use of the Lord's Prayer and the Ten Commandments. There is skimpy teaching on subjects such as tithing, forgiveness, honesty and especially holiness.

Many have not even heard of the Apostles' Creed, let alone memorized it. Folks are rushed into baptism without fully understanding the decision they have made. The baptism is fine, if teaching for new converts follows closely behind.

3. *No Deliverance Ministry*
   There are many "walking wounded" in the Church. Most churches do not have an effective deliverance ministry to minister to the needs of their people and the community. Some churches are like hospitals set up to comfort sick people rather than to heal them.

4. *Leaders Needing Deliverance*
   Unfortunately some clergy and leaders with demonic bondages have no help. There is just no one to turn to when leaders themselves need deliverance.

5. *Disbelief*
   Certain churches teach their people disbelief in the demonic. The people are taught that those things are not for today. Satan loves this one and does what he can to encourage such churches.

6. *Unprotected*
   Satanism, witchcraft and Freemasonry are alive and well and operative in our communities and even our churches. Christians desperately need education concerning the dangers and pitfalls of these issues. Many are unaware that there are specific assignments against some pastors and churches by witches and don't have the prayer protection or spiritual warfare tools to do effective combat.

7. *Unfinished Deliverance*
   Some churches with a deliverance ministry do only a partial job. As I mentioned above, if the whole personality is not ministered to, it is possible for demons to return and bring others.

there is hope

There is hope, however. Little by little the devil is beginning to overplay his hand. Society in general seems more open to the supernatural because of so much demonic emphasis in the movies and other media. There is an increasing frustration growing among Christian counselors who don't seem to be able to help some folks.

Church people are looking for better answers here and there. An excellent example of this is the Casas Adobes Baptist Church of Tucson, Arizona. Pastor Roger Barrier wrote the following in the winter 1999 issue of *Leadership* journal in an article entitled "When the Force Is Against You" (pp. 82-85):

> Today our church sponsors a deliverance ministry, which developed because of people who sought help for problems that could only be described as demonic. As we began caring for these folks, some in our congregation were upset. Some were convinced that demons existed only in the first-century world. Others were indignant; most were ignorant of spiritual warfare issues.
>
> A turning point was when our counseling pastor grew frustrated working with people who should have found emotional healing for their personal problems, reconciliation for their marriages, and harmony in their relationships—but never did. Well-trained by every secu-

lar standard in both counseling and psychology, our counseling pastor lamented that the success rate in the psychiatric field hovered around 10 percent.

When he added spiritual warfare to his tools for helping people, he discovered that people who were not helped in any other way began finding victory. When a problem does not yield to medical attention, standard psychological counseling, biblical insight, or the usual prayer requests, it is not unwise to consider the possibility of spiritual attack.

The only organized opposition I ever had against me the past 25 years of pastoring came from individuals who were dead set against our ministry to those harassed by the occult. I have learned to be patient in developing a spiritual warfare ministry within an established church. It needs to be done—but carefully and wisely.

But the ministry is worthwhile.

I worked for several hours with a woman who was spiritually overwhelmed. She hardly moved or changed facial expression as I demanded in the name of Christ that the numerous spirits who kept talking through her be silenced. I wanted to speak directly with her.

No one in the room that day will forget her face, frozen, locked in stone, a tear trickling out the corner of her left eye the moment I asked her if she wanted to receive Christ. Her lips moved and an almost imperceptible "yes" came out of her mouth.

Soon she was set free.

Few events demonstrate the power of God more than watching the Spirit of God overcome the forces of evil.

We desperately need to accelerate the training of staff to do deliverance in our churches. It is a hard job that can be demanding but at the same time rewarding. In my opinion, these need to be paid staff, because so many people needing and requesting deliverance are unable to pay. As Pastor Barrier said above, we can try the ordinary methods of prayer, counseling, biblical teaching and the like; but when all else fails, deliverance is probably the next step and we need a safe place to which people can be referred. Once there, the skills are needed to lead the ministry into "watching the Spirit of God overcome the forces of evil."

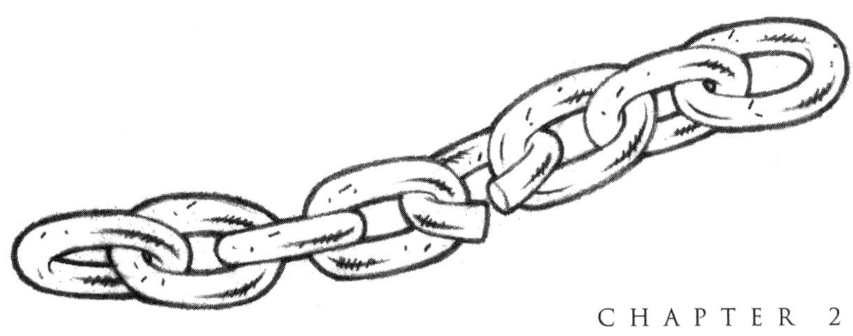

CHAPTER 2

who are these demons?

I do not pretend to be a theologian, but I am a practitioner. I always want to be sure that I agree with Scripture, but my bookish knowledge of demonology is not vast. I am more a person of faith and obedience than quantitative knowledge on the subject. I figure that if Jesus chose unlearned fishermen as His first students, it clearly demonstrates that vast theoretical knowledge may not be a prerequisite to the ministry of deliverance.

idols and demons

One morning I was reading in Deuteronomy 32 as my regular Bible reading. I was so sad to read in the Old Testament how God's chosen people would continually fall away and follow after idols or foreign gods time and again. Then verse 17 jumped out at me. It says, "They sacrificed to demons, not to God, to gods they did not know." I then looked up the word "demon" in our old Strong's Concordance and was shocked to discover that the word "demon" or "demons" is found only four times in the entire Old Testament. Each time it has to do with sacrificing to idols, indicating that those who sacrifice to idols are really sacrificing to demons. I concluded that idols apparently represent and might possibly embody demons.

The word "spirit" appears more often in the Old Testament and is frequently used in a negative way. I found, for example, lying spirits, familiar spirits, perverse spirits, distressing spirits, unclean spirits, spirits of harlotry, jealousy, heaviness, pride and ill will. Because of my practical experience over the years, I had run into all of these evil spirits many times and concluded that evil spirits and demons are one and the same. I haven't been able to find any remedy or way of dealing with evil spirits in the Old Testament, although I admit I may have missed something. At least, a remedy is not clear or common. Of course, not sacrificing to idols, which is commanded over and over, would at least be one way to avoid contact with demons.

Psalm 50:5 tells us a little more about sacrifices and what they do. It states, "Gather My saints together to Me, those who have made a covenant with Me by sacrifice." It could be concluded, therefore, that a sacrifice, especially one involving blood, produces a covenant which is a spiritual contract either with God or with demons. Since a covenant with God is a holy agreement, a covenant with demons produces an unholy agreement, and I would say a spiritual attachment with two-way communication occurs with both. Sacrifices are serious spiritual transactions between human beings and either the kingdom of darkness or the kingdom of light.

Just to bring this to a happy conclusion, let's think for a moment about Leviticus 17:11, which says, "For the life of the flesh is in the blood, and I have given it to you upon the altar to make atonement for your souls; for it is the blood that makes atonement for the soul." In my *New King James Version: The Open Bible Expanded Edition* (Nashville, TN: Thomas Nelson, 1985) the "Biblical Cyclopedic Index" defines the word "atonement" as "reconciliation of the guilty by divine sacrifice." How thankful we are that God made a way for us to be free of guilt for our sins through the sacrifice of Jesus!

Jesus changes the rules

As a matter of fact, things really changed with the coming of Christ. If I were teaching this to children, I would tell them that He left His holy place, where the devil couldn't touch Him, in order to come down to a place where He could do battle against the devil. It was sort of an open declaration of war.

After passing the test of the temptation in the wilderness, Jesus began to weaken the kingdom of darkness by casting out demons and showing His disciples how to do the same. In Mark 16:17,18 He even states, "These signs will follow those who believe. In My name they will cast out demons...they will lay hands on the sick and they will recover." That seems to include us, today. We should be continually pushing back the kingdom of darkness by being obedient to these orders.

The consensus among the authors I have read seems to be that demons are probably fallen angels with the assignment from their evil hierarchy to attach themselves to an individual and to eventually steal, kill or destroy (see John 10:10). They cannot attach themselves to a person without a cause, and we will examine that in detail later on. I just want to make it clear here that a Christian living a holy life doesn't usually need to worry about being demonized, in my opinion. By this I do not mean that Christians in general are exempt from demonic oppression, as we shall see shortly.

demons here and now

There was a time a few decades ago when it was suggested by pastors and teachers that there may have been demons on the mission field, but here in our Christian nation they weren't very prevalent. But times are changing. I am writing this in the month of May 1999, and twice this month our local secular Colorado Springs newspaper carried articles that mentioned the word "demon."

On May 11, *The Gazette* carried a story about a seven-year-old boy named Jonathan who "is affectionate and gives lots of hugs. Then in an instant something inside him changes. Jonathan transforms into a raging demon, biting, hitting and kicking those around him while screaming and throwing whatever he can get his hands on. The fit usually lasts about 10 minutes." It was also mentioned that Jonathan was an adopted child. The diagnosis was that he was a kid with a combination of developmental and mental disorders, often referred to as a serious emotional disturbance. The article went on to say that these kids are often the cause of broken friendships and marriages and frequently end up in jail.

On May 21, *The Gazette* front-page story carried the other mention of the word "demon." None other than President Clinton made it as he met with the parents of the murdered Columbine High School victims, wounded survivors and their families. The headline read, "'Dark Forces' Swept Over Killers, President Says." The article went on to explain, in part: "In the role of national healer, which Clinton said he had assumed all too often in his six years as President, he also extended some compassion to the killers, saying their struggle with demons is a universal one. 'These dark forces that take over people and make them murder are the extreme manifestation of fear and rage with which every human has to do combat.'"

The negative influences of the media, movie and television industries; "dark" novels; video games with demonic themes; and other such things bring the thought of evil forces and demons close to home and, in many instances, right into some homes. So the word "demon" is now more common and its true meaning is more accepted than it was a generation ago.

Now comes the scary part. *Leadership* journal carried an article in the fall 1995 issue by Michael Sack in which he states, "I've been researching Americans' sense of what is evil and found that in large part we have lost a concrete definition for it. Generation X, for example, has almost no concept of evil. Political correctness requires that people consider all ideas equally. In doing so, we lose our sense of right and wrong. The group under 25 has refined this process to an art."

Because of the negative influences mentioned above, as well as having lost a sense of right and wrong, we see evolving a generation of youngsters who are highly disadvantaged. As I mentioned in the introduction, because of an extremely high divorce rate, fatherless homes are more prevalent in the current generation. The permissiveness of our present-day secular culture, hostility toward teaching morals through such simple things as the Ten Commandments in schoolrooms, heavy-metal music encouraging sinful thoughts and behavior, and the agenda of the homosexual community seeking to force their values on society all contribute to disadvantage a generation. This all adds up to making it easy to pick up or invite demonic activity in great abundance in this generation.

Therefore, the Church needs to equip itself thoroughly and quickly to address the issues at hand. These above-mentioned problems are greatly exaggerated in some places more than in others; for example, in inner city settings high crime and drugs are added to the mix. Christian workers have one hand tied behind their backs if they are unaware of deliverance ministries and techniques.

My conclusion: Yes, evil spirits are out there seeking to take advantage of individuals and are infesting this generation as never before. We must be salt and light to the world and not be afraid to learn about demons and what to do about them. The answer is simple but requires equipping and action. Jesus said to cast out demons and He has given us two tools: His authority and His name. Those who choose to take up the task must be living holy lives free from all known sin. God honors our feeble attempts at deliverance, and skill comes with practice, just as with any art or craft—the more you do it, the better you get at it.

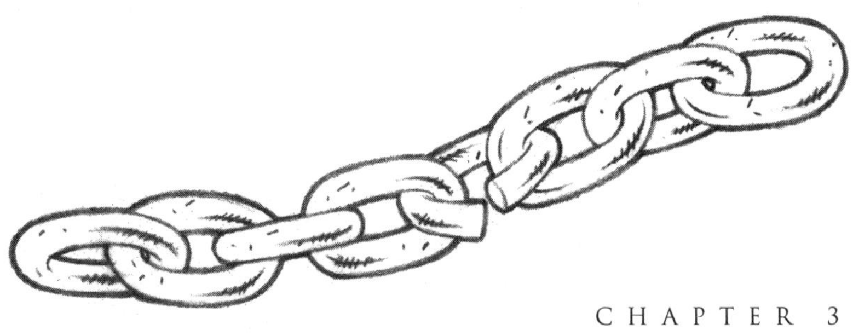

CHAPTER 3

deliverance evangelism

How do demons gain entrance into an individual's life?

body, soul and spirit

First of all, let's take a look at the makeup of a person. Most deliverance practitioners agree that humans consist of three parts as succinctly described in 1 Thessalonians 5:23: "Now may the God of peace sanctify you completely and may your whole spirit, soul, and body be preserved blameless at the coming of our Lord Jesus Christ."

The body is what we see when we look at a person. We see such things as the person's hair, eyes and skin color, whether the person is male or female, tall or short, fat or skinny, young or old, athletic or handicapped and so forth. But we all know that is not the real person—it's just the handy shell that houses the real individual. It helps us to tell one from the other because so few people look exactly alike. I never cease to marvel at the creativity of the Lord in designing noses, eyes, chins, foreheads and other facial features.

The spirit is the portion of a person that lives forever—it's the life that God breathed into Adam as described in Genesis 2:7. It has also been described by many as the residence of the Holy Spirit when regeneration takes place.

The soul of a person is more complex. It houses such things as the emotions, mind, will, five senses and personality. It is from the soul that the real person, personality and behavior come forth. I believe that Satan can bring bondage to the body at times. Jesus mentions a "spirit of infirmity" in Luke 13:11,12 that caused a woman to be bent over for 18 years. More common, however, are bondages that afflict the soul, usually involving an emotion such as hatred or a behavior such as an addiction. David says in Psalm 41:4, "Heal my soul for I have sinned against you." This seems to imply that some bad choice was made that brought a problem to David's soul, and it seemed to have lingered until David asked for its removal.

Christians need deliverance, too

The big question that I always get is, "Can a Christian be demon possessed?"

In my experience, the answer to that is no. The next question is, "Can a Christian have a demonic bondage?" My answer to that is most definitely, yes.

I pray deliverance only for Christians. I believe that a person needs the power of the Holy Spirit to maintain deliverance. From the testimonies of those whom I have prayed for, it is rather easy to maintain deliverance with the help of the Holy

Spirit once the demon has been expelled. The testimonies sound quite similar and include statements like, "How wonderful it is to experience normal temptation that comes from the outside instead of the kind that rages uncontrollably from within and can't be withstood."

deliverance for unbelievers

However, demonic deliverance can also be focused on unbelievers when it is accompanied by aggressive evangelism. If they do not receive Christ and invite the Holy Spirit into their lives, however, the demons will come back, often bringing more with them.

As mentioned before, Peter and I spent a good chunk of our adult lives as missionaries in Latin America. We wish that we knew then what we know now, because we would have done a much better job. But we can't relive the past and we were doing the best we could with what we had at the time. God has graciously given us the wonderful opportunity of preparing missionaries to do a whole lot better than we did by showing them how to avoid the many mistakes that we made.

We frequently go back to Latin America and have made many ministry trips there since moving back to the U.S. in 1971. Overall, the Church in Latin America has a greater understanding about deliverance and what I will term "deliverance evangelism." There has been a great move of the Spirit over the past 20 years in many nations, notably Argentina, Guatemala, Brazil and Colombia, with many other nations close behind. Some term the movement a "revival." If it isn't a revival, it is pretty close! We can learn a great deal about deliverance evangelism from them.

when witchcraft becomes an issue

It is interesting to note that overt witchcraft in various and sundry forms is very prevalent throughout Latin America. People are in tune with spiritual power. Folk religions continue in strength especially among the indigenous population, and it is very common to consult with *curanderos,* or witch doctors, who deal with dark spiritual powers. So evil spirits are not something unfamiliar, like tales from a faraway country. One can readily locate shops that sell all sorts of witchcraft paraphernalia, and witches are available to assist with curses, spells and other requests in their business. When I was in Argentina, I even saw an article in a magazine about the president's private witch and how he consulted her from time to time for help. It had pictures of her "office" that sent chills down my spine.

Carlos Annacondia, of Argentina, is a longtime friend who is gaining an international reputation as an extremely effective evangelist. His recent book *Listen to Me, Satan!* (Lake Mary, FL: Creation House, 1998) is well worth reading. In this book he gives his testimony and explains how he uses deliverance evangelism in his campaigns.

Carlos is a humble businessman who runs a factory that manufactures literal nuts and bolts. He has had only a sixth-grade education because he had to go to work to help support his family at an early age. When he was saved, he began to study the Bible fervently and soon had a gift of faith that wouldn't quit. I love to be around him because that faith is highly contagious and I enjoy catching a good case of it every now and then.

Carlos began to pray for the sick, simply because the Bible said to, and he saw immediate and dramatic results. He soon began preaching, and people came to the Lord in large numbers. He then embarked upon some evangelistic campaigns which he funded himself and he has since traveled all over Argentina, Latin America, Europe, Asia and North America. Let me describe the scenario of one of his campaigns—I've been there.

He will typically rent a large, vacant lot and set up a huge electric generator, a high, large platform and several hundred chairs that are placed some distance from the platform in order to allow for people flow closer toward the front when the altar call is made. These chairs are used only for the sick, elderly or handicapped. Everyone else stands throughout the whole meeting.

The platform is high, not only so that the crowd can get a better view, but to accommodate a large team of intercessors to pray beneath the platform throughout the meeting. The platform is draped in cloth so they are hidden. When Carlos feels like he needs a special dose of fervent prayer because of something he is seeing or sensing, he simply taps a signal on the platform floor. A typical campaign will last a month or more, as the Lord leads. Carlos works in his factory by day and holds his campaigns at night. He will usually go to dinner around midnight or later. Peter and I got up from the dinner table with him at 3:45 A.M. on one occasion!

annacondia blends deliverance with evangelism

But there is one other piece of equipment that I have never seen at any other campaign anywhere. It is a huge tent, placed about 30 feet from the platform and behind Carlos's back when he is preaching to the crowd. Inside this tent are many groups of three chairs all facing one another. This is what he calls his "Spiritual Intensive Care Unit," and its sole purpose is deliverance.

He hired his barber, a guitar player, and a very gifted deliverance worker named Pablo Bottari to manage the deliverance tent.

Pablo will go to the city where Carlos has scheduled a campaign. It should be mentioned here that the campaigns are so effective that the entire religious climate of a city will often be changed for the good, and churches will suddenly burst at the seams with the many new converts. It is not uncommon to hear the phrases "before Annacondia" and "after Annacondia" when describing a church in a city. Churches gladly welcome a campaign and freely offer ushers, helpers of all sorts and counselors for the deliverance tent. Pablo trains the counselors, many of whom are blue-collar workers who have worked all day. But when Carlos gets to go to dinner after midnight, these counselors are often just getting started on their deliverance work and will stay all night if needed. Their job is to lead the people to Christ and get them delivered. Sleep is a luxury that just has to wait until the job is done.

How are the persons selected for the deliverance tent? Carlos simply starts a prayer in his service with the title of his abovementioned book by shouting, "Listen to me, Satan, and listen to me good!" As the prayer progresses, demons begin to manifest all over the audience. Many people will fall writhing to the ground, kicking and screaming as the demons who have tormented them in the past begin to manifest. Carlos seems to almost taunt them into manifesting, but it is for a purpose—so that the demonized persons are singled out and can receive help.

A TEAM OF "STRETCHER BEARERS"

Stationed throughout the crowd (and it is not unusual to have up to 20,000 people in populous areas) are well-trained "stretcher bearers." It is the task of these men to locate the demonized individuals and carefully transport them back to the tent. There will already be two counselors seated in the tent, and the stretcher bearers will place a person in the third chair. They will return to the crowd, and the work of the counselors begins. Only one person at a time deals with the afflicted person while the other one prays. They take turns when necessary or when weariness sets in.

One more group of people quietly passes through the crowd. These are ladies with shopping bags who pick up shoes, eyeglasses, purses and anything else left behind by the manifesting individuals. They go back to the tent when the bag is full and match up the shoes in their bag with those wearing only one shoe. They bring together the owners and the lost and found items as best they can. This brigade of servants brought a smile to my lips. They have thought of everything!

Think of the fallout of this system. How many thousands of laypeople have been trained in deliverance and continue casting out demons after Annacondia leaves? How many people have found Christ and been cleansed of demons in one fell swoop? How many true "power encounters" have taken place in which the powers of evil have come face-to-face with the power of the Holy Spirit? How many times has there been someone available to pray for and deliver the person, seeing that one through to faith, cleansing and a dramatically changed life? I think we have something to learn here.

As the crusade advances, a few of those who have been healed, saved and delivered give brief testimonies of what the Lord did for them. In the audience will be some unsaved relatives and friends of these people who hear simple, unpolished but fresh testimonies of how the Lord has changed their lives. This is powerful fuel to pour on the revival fire.

This is deliverance evangelism at its finest and most developed, in spite of the crude outdoor environment. People will stand in the rain or bitter cold throughout a meeting because revival doesn't wait for sunshine or the stars. Spiritual hunger wants spiritual food *now*.

césar castellanos of bogotá

Here is one final story I will share with you about what to do with new converts. It is impressive to me because, once again, it involves another friend, César Castellanos. I can't help throwing in these personal asides because they are so close to our hearts.

We labored in Latin America in the tough days when the growth of the Church was slow and costly. To see the Church burst into bloom and for the Lord to allow us to live to observe it is such a joy. Most of the younger, dynamic pastors were converted and raised up into ministry without the help of missionaries, and the Church is rapidly coming into its own without outside help. Missionaries are going out from Latin America to difficult places in the world to evangelize, so missions has come full circle.

Just two years ago we were battling in prayer for César's life.

He is a fairly young man with a huge, growing church in Bogotá. His lovely, dynamic wife, Claudia, has already served in the national Senate (the only pregnant senator Colombia has had to date). She was largely responsible for pushing through the rewriting of the constitution to include religious liberty. Protestants were subject to severe discrimination before Claudia's bold move. Colombia has a reputation concerning drug trafficking, and the cartels are powerful, wealthy and feared. Death squads appear now and then, having been hired by criminals or possibly politicians and death threats are fairly common. César and Claudia had received several death threats because they had a reputation for being anti-crime. Homeowners often hire armed guards, and kidnapping for ransom happens weekly. So, this fills you in on some of the background.

GUNNED DOWN BY THE ENEMY

A little over two years ago, César and Claudia were taking their grade-school daughter and six of her little girlfriends to a restaurant for her birthday party after church one Sunday noon. While stopped at a red light, they were savagely attacked by a gunman on the back of a motorcycle with an automatic gun. When the rain of bullets ceased and the attacker sped away, the seven girls were totally unharmed but had witnessed the brutality of seeing Claudia wounded twice, in the chest and in the thigh. Miraculously, vital organs had been missed.

César took six bullets in the upper part of his body, one of which penetrated a lung and the other narrowly missing his jugular veins and spinal cord. They were rushed to the hospital, and Claudia was treated and released in a few days. However, César hovered between life and death for days. Infection set in his lung and his trachea was badly damaged. Upon his release from intensive care, he and Claudia came to the United States for some weeks of further repair and recuperation as death threats continued to arrive at their church. After a couple of months, they boldly returned to Bogotá and César resumed his preaching with his voice totally restored.

In the midst of this, the church is thriving. As a matter of fact, the city of Cali has the largest quarterly prayer meeting we know about. All of the Protestant churches join together and fill a 55,000-seat stadium for an all-night prayer meeting. The last prayer meeting not only filled the stadium, but thousands were unable to get in as the seats were filled. And, yes, they do pray all night!

the three-day retreat

All that to say this: *New Wine* magazine carried this report dated July 22, 1998, entitled "Church Growth in Bogotá, Colombia." Ken Gott reported about the world's fastest growing church in Bogotá, Colombia:

> Pastor Castellanos' church is expected to have 50,000 home groups by the end of the year. His youth go to church on Saturday to make room for everybody else on Sundays. But instead of doing nothing, the 50,000 youth line the roads in groups of 100s and pray over all the cars going to church! This church uses a model that involves taking every new convert for a three-day retreat. Here they make sure they understand what they've done and pray for deliverance from demons and family curses, then pray for physical healings, for the baptism of the Spirit, for anointing, and teach them the basic doctrines of the church. All in three days right after getting saved!

The point I wish to emphasize is that if deliverance is carried out at the time of conversion or shortly thereafter, it is my guess that it can be a great factor in evangelism and in sustaining a revival for the vigorous growth of the Church. At the time of this writing, the Argentine revival is now in its seventeenth year and that is an astoundingly long revival. The leaders affirm that deliverance plays a very important role in sustaining that revival.

Now, let's join in getting some teaching that would be useful if you were ever called upon to work in a "deliverance tent."

clues indicating possible demonic presence

What are some of the most common clues that indicate the possibility of the presence of a demon in the life of an individual? By the way, the best words to use are "afflicted," "in bondage," "oppressed," "demonized," and in severe cases "tormented." The most common word nowadays is "demonized," and it denotes that there is a presence there, but it certainly is not demon possession when it comes to a Christian. It is more like a demon attaches itself to something, such as a recurring bad habit, and has reason to be there. I will list five here:

1. *No Personal Control*

   Is the person totally in control, or does the phrase continually repeat, "I have prayed and confessed and cried but I cannot get the victory over this besetting sin." When praying, confessing and crying are not quite enough, it is a pretty good clue that perhaps a demonic presence is involved. In other words, the person does not control that particular problem, but the problem controls the person.

2. *Sense of Helplessness*

   Similar to point one above, not only a feeling of helplessness but one of hopelessness also sets in. It could be something like hatred toward a person who wronged you and whenever the thought comes to mind or you see a picture of the person, the emotion boils up once again. Even after confessing it to the Lord, it just won't go away permanently.

3. *Something Comes Over the Person*
   This is a pretty telltale symptom. Remember little seven-year-old Jonathan in the last chapter who is sweet as sugar until he suddenly transforms into a "raging demon"? A person can be in one frame of mind one moment and then, like the sudden switch of a light going off, darkness overtakes the person. Something "engages," causing a totally different frame of mind to kick in, and generally the person gets out of control in some emotional area or behavioral action.

4. *A Voice Says to Do Something Terrible*
   Usually the voice tells the person to commit suicide or some violent act. Experts have told me that some mental illnesses can be accompanied by voices that are not necessarily demonic in nature. But when the voice tells the person to do something clearly sinful, evil or deadly, I would certainly investigate the possibility of demonic activity.

5. *Past Involvement with Occultic Groups*
   These groups range from engaging in the worship of a deity other than Jehovah God and His Son, Jesus Christ, to making use of magic or curses to harm others.

   Seeing the word "Freemasonry" in this list comes as a shock to many people who have come to believe that Freemasonry is just a helpful civic organization. This is not so. A strong case can be made for the fact that it is a non-Christian religion. Appendix 5 to this book is "A Prayer of Release for Freemasons and Their Descendants." Unholy vows and covenants are made that are demonic in nature and provide openings for

> curses. As a matter of fact, I highly recommend a very excellent book entitled *Evicting Demonic Intruders* by Noel and Phyl Gibson (Ventura, CA: Regal Books, 1993). There is an entire chapter entitled "Freemasons Curse Themselves, Their Families and Their Churches." It is a very enlightening chapter. Finally, the above-mentioned Prayer of Release listed in appendix 5 has a good bibliography written from a Christian perspective with many resources.
>
> The main reason we include involvement in witchcraft and satanism is that these activities involve curses and open invitations to demons, either directly or indirectly. These curses and activities must be renounced and broken in the name of Jesus and by His blood. Then, demons can be evicted. More about that later.

In deliverance, we always work backward, asking the questions, What seems to be the problem and when did it first start? Now, let's examine possible entry points that allow demons access.

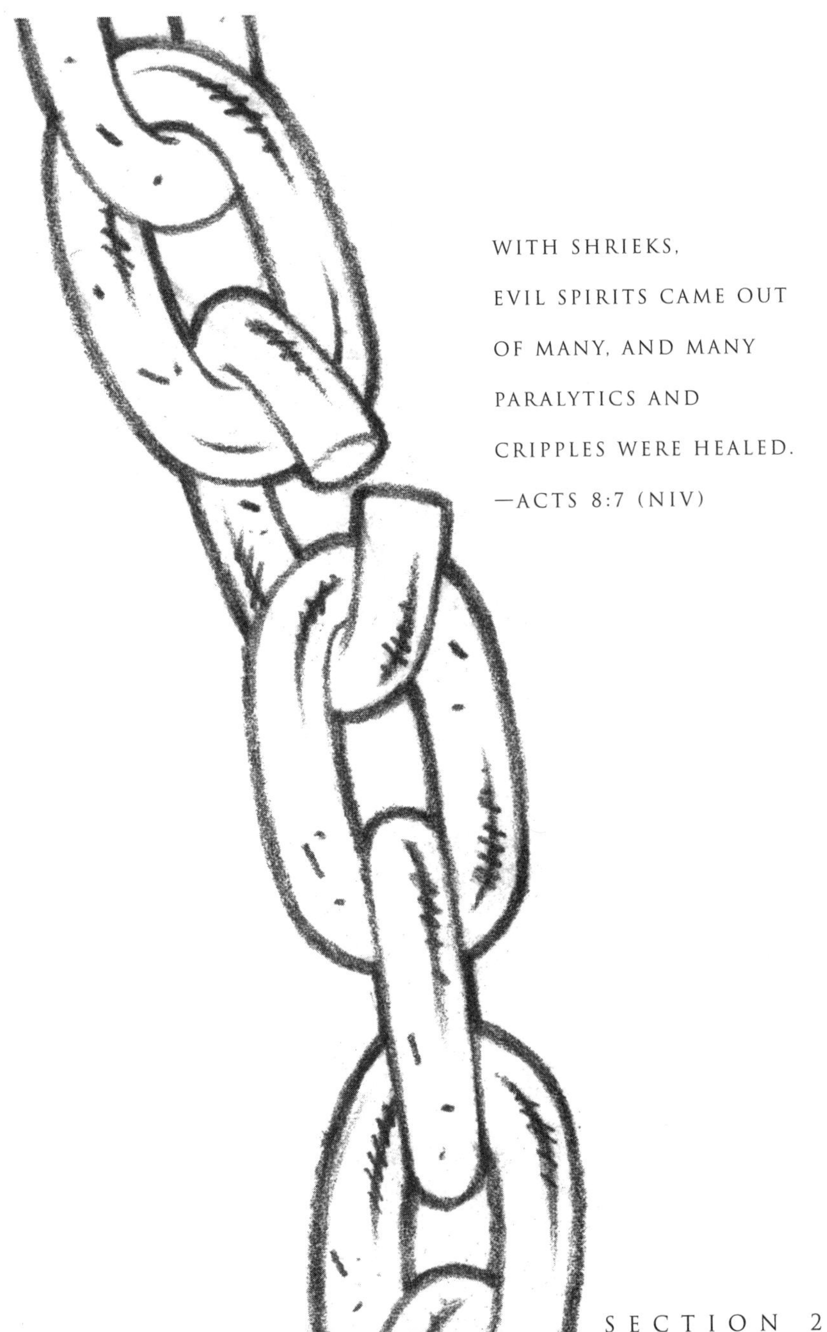

WITH SHRIEKS,
EVIL SPIRITS CAME OUT
OF MANY, AND MANY
PARALYTICS AND
CRIPPLES WERE HEALED.
—ACTS 8:7 (NIV)

SECTION 2

demonic entry points

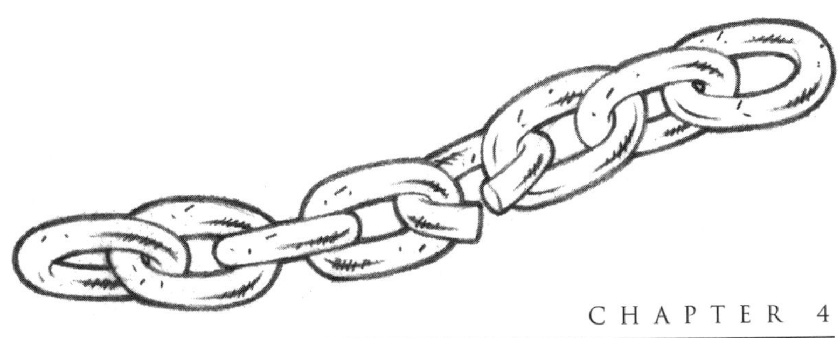

CHAPTER 4

hereditary spirits

roots of destructive behaviors in families

I will probably repeat several times during the course of this basic manual that we always work backward in deliverance. In the last chapter, we discussed clues that indicate the possible presence of demons oppressing an individual. In this chapter, we will discuss the possibility of hereditary spirits as the demonic entry point in a person's life.

a dad controlled by rage

Let's suppose that a man shows up on your doorstep requesting prayer for a problem with uncontrollable rage. He confides in you that he is a dad who, when disciplining a child, begins to shake the child and can't stop. With tears streaming down his cheeks, he confesses that he is afraid he will kill his own son someday if he does not get help.

Uncontrollable rage is the symptom. If he is not in control, but something is spurring him on to this undesired action, we have a good clue that there is probably demonic activity at work because he is unable to stop the behavior.

The next question is, Why is it there? I will try to answer this as simply as I can.

Demons take advantage of many things that cause severe hurt or trauma to a person and this is what they attach themselves to. There is always a reason for them to be present. I will list a few of the most common entry points that I have encountered while praying for hundreds of people over the years. What I am calling an entry point others may call a "foothold," "stronghold," "root" or some other similar term.

Let's get back to the dad in the first paragraph. He is suffering from a spirit of rage, often connected with a spirit of violence. We look for some incident in his life that might have opened him up to one or both of these things. We would ask if he was treated just like that as a child by either of his parents, grandparents, a close relative, or if violent behavior was talked about a lot as having been common in the "family tree." We are fishing here for what we would call an inherited or generational spirit, especially if a parent or grandparent or close relative was involved. I would thoroughly explore this possibility first.

If that comes up negative, I would look for violent acts committed against him or in which he was involved, such as being a member of a violent gang or fighting in a war where violence surrounded him. Another possibility might be martial arts, a well-known door opener for a spirit of violence. A fascination with violent, demonic video games and an insatiable thirst for playing them or war games, or enjoying watching violent movies and TV shows can also be an entry point. A traumatic, violent act committed against the man when he was young might also have opened the door to this problem.

familial spirits and familiar spirits

We need to discuss the generational or inherited spirit at this point. This spirit is also called a "familial spirit," and some deliverance practitioners call it a "familiar spirit." I don't use those two terms much because they sound so alike that I find it confusing, but let me explain the difference between the two as I see it. I believe the correct one of the two terms to use when referring to a generational spirit is a "familial spirit," as in something found in a family line. *The Random House Dictionary of the English Language* (New York, NY: Random House, 1967) defines the word "familial" as "pertaining to or characteristic of a family" or "appearing in individuals by heredity." This seems to fit the case.

The phrase "familiar spirit" (or spirits) occurs 16 times in my concordance and each time has to do with witches, sorcerers, diviners, wizards or some other form of the occult. I believe especially New Age advocates call this same spirit a "spirit guide" nowadays. This happens when an individual has come up against problems too large or complex to easily work out and then asks for a "spirit guide" to help make decisions or to provide spiritual guidance for him or her. This is an invited demonic spirit that the person is then incapable of uninviting, because the foothold has been established. It is a very controlling spirit and can become very tormenting. I was fascinated to find "familiar spirit" listed in my unabridged dictionary and defined as "a supernatural spirit or demon supposed to attend on or serve a person." It is a pretty accurate description of what I am talking about in this paragraph.

a spirit guide

The winter 1999 issue of *Leadership* journal carried a very interesting article by Roger Barrier entitled "When the Force is Against You—Battling Spiritual Oppression." (Roger is a Baptist pastor in Tucson, Arizona.) Here is a brief excerpt from page 85 that clearly illustrates a spirit guide:

> The man from the utility company finished his work and said, "You're Roger Barrier, aren't you? I listen to your radio program every day. My wife and I are both Christians. She's having some problems; in fact there are times when I wonder what's going on inside of her. Do you believe in demons?"
>
> "Yes," I replied. "Why don't we sit down in the kitchen and talk?"
>
> "Several months ago," he began, "we went to a spiritualist church where we were encouraged to pray to receive spirit guides to help direct our lives. I didn't pray for any, but my wife did. She hasn't been the same since.
>
> "Sometimes, it's as if there's a different person inside. Her voice changes; her face contorts; she has an aversion to the things of God. Our marriage is falling apart. She won't go back to our Christian church.
>
> "It all came to a head last night. While we were arguing, she walked into the hallway, turned slowly, and said with a sneer, 'Don't you know who we are?' Her voice rose to a scream as she repeated, 'Don't you know who we are? Don't you know who we are?'"
>
> He was shaking now.
>
> "I think," he said, "she is demon possessed like they talk about in the Bible. Can you help us?"

The author goes on to share how he set up a deliverance ministry in his church because he found a need and was willing to learn how to help.

One more warning about spirit guides. We must keep a sharp lookout for the agenda of the New Age group who seeks to infiltrate our schools with this demonic practice. When we were living in California, it came to the attention of some of our Christian teachers that there was an attempt to push new curriculum into the grade schools. It encouraged the small children to ask the help of an imaginary friend to accompany them and help them make decisions. Can you see how that could easily be an opening for a familiar spirit to be invited into the life of an innocent child and then influence that youngster to make all sorts of decisions that could harm him or her? Fortunately, at that time, parents blew the whistle and the curriculum was rejected. I don't know if they tried again. We just can't take for granted that our schools teach wholesome things that meet with our approval. Keep a close eye on what happens there!

Let's get back to our dad suffering from uncontrollable rage. Suppose that we have tried all of the above and we discover that this dad did, indeed, fight in a war and witnessed killings and atrocities that left him emotionally scarred. If this is the only one that is answered positively out of all of the questions asked, we then address the problem by name. This is how I would pray: "And now, in the name of Jesus Christ, you spirit of rage, I bind you, I break your power, and I command you to loose John and let him go *now*!" I also would pray the same prayer addressing a spirit of violence. The two usually go together.

I will give you examples such as this several times over so that you become comfortable with praying these prayers of command and they become like formulas to you in case they are needed in a hurry someday. You will find it strange that because you have some of this information stored up, an opportunity to use it just might present itself someday soon!

frequently encountered generational spirits

Now to our first specific entry point, that of inherited problems. These are usually called generational, or hereditary, spirits. There seem to be certain spirits that are assigned to family lines because someone in the past opened up the door for them. I will name a few.

1. *Spirit of Rejection*

   This probably tops the list of hereditary spirits: I have prayed for many people who have felt emotionally abandoned by their parents. Upon further investigation, it was discovered that the parents treated the person I was praying for exactly as they themselves had been treated while growing up. "Like begets like." While it is understandable and explainable, it doesn't take the hurt away, and the emotion of rejection must be dealt with.

   Hereditary rejection frequently manifests with physical abuse of some sort. When this surfaces, it is usually apparent that the abuser has also been abused, often in the same way. If the abused was beaten, typically his or her parents also beat the abuser, and sometimes this goes back for several generations. When this spirit is in the family line, the normal response on the part of the parents is frustration, anger and disappointment; and their method of discipline is to beat the tar out of a kid until blood flows or black and blue marks are left for days.

2. *Suicide, Anxiety and Depression*
   These problems can often be traced to deeper issues in family lines. Remember that when any emotional or mental problem turns up, the next thing to do is to delve into family history. If the identical problem afflicted a family member in a previous generation, then you must first address that generational spirit by name before addressing the spirit that is currently troubling the person. In other words, you need to address the two separate spirits.

3. *Spirit of Lust*
   Lust is another common generational spirit. "My father had an affair, my grandmother wasn't faithful to Grandpa, and Uncle Harry ran a porn shop" would be clues to a generational spirit of lust that has been passed down. By this I mean that early in life a youngster would have symptoms which indicate that lust might be an ongoing problem. I have prayed for men who were bothered by compulsive masturbation since their earliest memories. This is abnormal. It's not hard to figure out that they had some "help" with this habit. When a problem like this appears at an early age, we look for a generational spirit that is trying to get the person hooked on something very young in life. Hereditary spirits of lust seem to draw others who have the same problem, since "birds of a feather flock together."

4. *Ancestral Involvement with Palm Reading or Astrology*
   Such practices may have allowed witchcraft into a family line. Witchcraft is particularly strong; and there are generally curses, spells and unholy covenants that affect children born into these families. Satan is especially interested in tampering with children so that they are in misery the rest of their lives. His self-appointed job, remember, is to steal, kill and destroy. The earlier he can gain entrance, the more he can steal, destroy and sometimes eventually kill. Nothing pleases him more than abortion. If he can kill a child before it has drawn its first breath, his job is that much easier. This is, of course, my personal opinion, but it's a very strong one.

   Persons with this generational spirit will find themselves drawn to psychics, magic, astral travel, New Age, necromancy, tarot cards, the *Ouija* board, horoscopes, seances, astrology and many other related activities.

5. *Spirit of Addiction*
   It will come as no surprise to you that certain problems seem to follow family lines. Addictions to things such as alcohol, drugs, gambling, overspending, compulsive exercise, food, caffeine and the like are commonly known to run in families. A spirit of addiction can take on many forms and still be the same spirit. For example, a mom may have a problem with alcoholism, but her son may be afflicted with an addiction to drugs if alcoholism has not hooked him.

I have listed some of the most common hereditary spirits. How do I deal with them when their cover has been blown? The answer is, usually, first. This is a crucial beginning point.

It is often a bit of a relief for a person to know that if the problem started very early on, an opening was probably made in the family line by some relative in a former generation. The person had some ungodly help nudging him or her on toward the problem. Let's take, for example, a generational spirit of rejection, accompanied by physical abuse. How would I begin working with a man who had been severely abused by his father?

forgiveness as a weapon in deliverance

I have chosen the words of the above subtitle very carefully. I spoke previously about two weapons Jesus gave to His followers to accomplish His command to cast out demons. These are His authority and His name. I also believe that one of the greatest weapons He has given to the person in bondage is that of forgiveness. Let me explain.

The first thing I would ask the man would be something like, "Was your father himself abused by his parents?" Because this is usually the case, it would then be appropriate for him to pray, stating that he forgives the guilty person who created the opening in the family line. I would then ask him to pray, telling the Lord that he forgives his father for the severe physical and emotional abuse he received at his hand. Sometimes this is hard to do, especially if the abuse was severe and prolonged. Bitter tears often accompany the prayer of forgiveness as painful memories come to mind. Always have plenty of tissues and a wastebasket available.

If I see that the person is having trouble forgiving, I can generally encourage him or her to pray something like, "As Christ forgave my sin, I also choose to forgive my father for the physical and emotional abuse I suffered as a child and teenager." I tell them that *forgiveness is a choice, not a feeling*. Yes, what he did was wrong and, yes, it hurt physically and emotionally. Forgiveness does not condone the action; it just removes the sting and the legal right for the hereditary spirit to hang in there for another generation. Forgiveness must be extended first so that the legal right is removed from the scene. The "legal right" is defined as that which "feeds" the demon and gives it permission to remain. Once the person forgives the perpetrator, the legal right for the demon to stay has been removed, and it must leave when commanded to do so.

Take the time to reread the preceding paragraph. It is one of the most important things you will learn if you have not been exposed to this teaching before. Let's talk about forgiveness a little more.

Forgiveness is a concept that is quite foreign to most of the other major religions of the world. It isn't even stressed a whole lot in the Jewish tradition as described in the Old Testament, but it is there. However, when Christ comes along, He ushers in a whole new emphasis on kind behavior, especially forgiveness. His followers had to understand the concepts of guilt and forgiveness so they would understand what was happening through the crucifixion.

When the disciples asked Jesus to teach them to pray, He did so by giving them the Lord's Prayer. It is interesting to me that profound doctrine is mentioned throughout that prayer, but only one of the themes is strongly reiterated—that of forgiveness. The verses that follow declare: "For if you forgive men their trespasses, your heavenly Father will also forgive you. But if you do not forgive men their trespasses, neither will your Father forgive your trespasses" (Matt. 6:14,15).

the power of the *Jesus* film

I delight in following the progress of the use of Campus Crusade's *Jesus* film. It is one of the greatest tools on planet Earth in the evangelism of unreached people groups. It is a very tastefully done film, but what gives it supernatural power is that it has no written narration added. It uses only the God-inspired narration found in the book of Luke.

I recently received a press release from the Campus Crusade office in Orlando, Florida, that contained a portion of a speech made by Bill Bright, founder of Campus Crusade. Among other things, he is quoted as saying,

> Our great, wonderful Lord is calling the Muslim world to Himself. Perhaps you already know that Islamic theology has no place for forgiveness. Islam is primarily law, legalism, punishment, death, and vengeance. That is why they are stunned, even troubled, for days after they view the *Jesus* film.
>
> When they learn of Jesus' life of love and forgiveness, they are drawn to Him. The concepts in the film are so foreign that sometimes Muslims ask to see *Jesus* two and three times before they grasp what it means. Amazingly, they readily accept His miracles as historical fact and are deeply impressed. But they are moved most by His forgiveness, that He willingly carried His cross for them, and then died on it, taking upon Himself His Father's vengeance...for their sins. For them, it is truly a revolutionary concept."

Unforgiveness creates bondage. Bondage is like a rope that ties up two things, in this case two persons: the one who was wronged and the one who committed the wrong. But a wonderful thing happens in the human spirit when forgiveness is extended. It frees *two* people. I can't tell you how many times I have heard back from someone I've prayed with who had a serious problem involving unforgiveness. Mind you, the guilty person is not excused for wrongdoing, just forgiven. But the guilty person is also thereby freed and enabled to act differently because he or she is no longer bound to someone else's unforgiveness. Apologies are often forthcoming from someone who hadn't been heard from in years. A card saying "I love you" will come from someone who never said it before in his or her life. That somehow covers me with a major warm, pink fuzzy!

When the prayer of forgiveness is finished, I address the generational spirit. "And now, you hereditary spirit of rejection," I say, "your assignment over this person is *over*; and in the name of Jesus Christ, I command you to loose this brother and let him go now; and I forbid you to go on to his children!" Even if the person is single and has no children, I pray for any unborn children, so the trait is cut off from the family line in the name of Jesus.

spirits can team up

We are dealing with a minimum of two demonic spirits when generational spirits pop up. One is the generational spirit itself and the other is the spirit that the person has either invited into his or her life, both by the same name. In the above-mentioned case involving a hereditary spirit of rejection, the person has also picked up a second spirit of rejection by being a victim. So *that* spirit of rejection must also be evicted. Often spirits of perceived rejection and fear of rejection accompany this group. I always mention all four of them when praying over rejection issues, and we will spend more time dealing with root causes of rejection in the next chapter. Learn these well, because I have found that they usually accompany every deliverance assignment in some form or other.

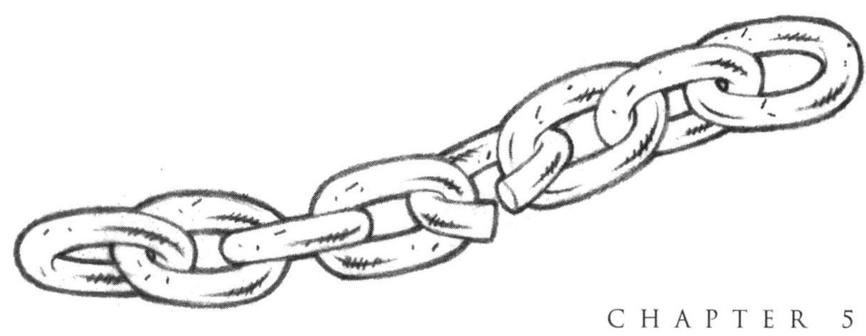

CHAPTER 5

rejection

abandonment, inferiority, guilt and shame

I am deeply indebted to Noel and Phyl Gibson of Australia, who taught me almost everything I know, mostly through their books but occasionally by fax and letter. Noel is at home with the Lord now.

A copy of one of the helps that they produced in their excellent book *Evicting Demonic Intruders* (Ventura, CA: Renew Books, 1993) was on my lap at all times as I prayed deliverance for the first few years. I am grateful that I was granted permission to use it throughout the book. If it will help you, copy it and put it on your lap as well. The Gibsons entitle it "The Root and Fruit Systems of Rejection." For short, I will call it the "rejection tree."

roots on the rejection tree

Let me explain the tree very simply. Remember, "root produces fruit." Using our "working backward" model, when a person

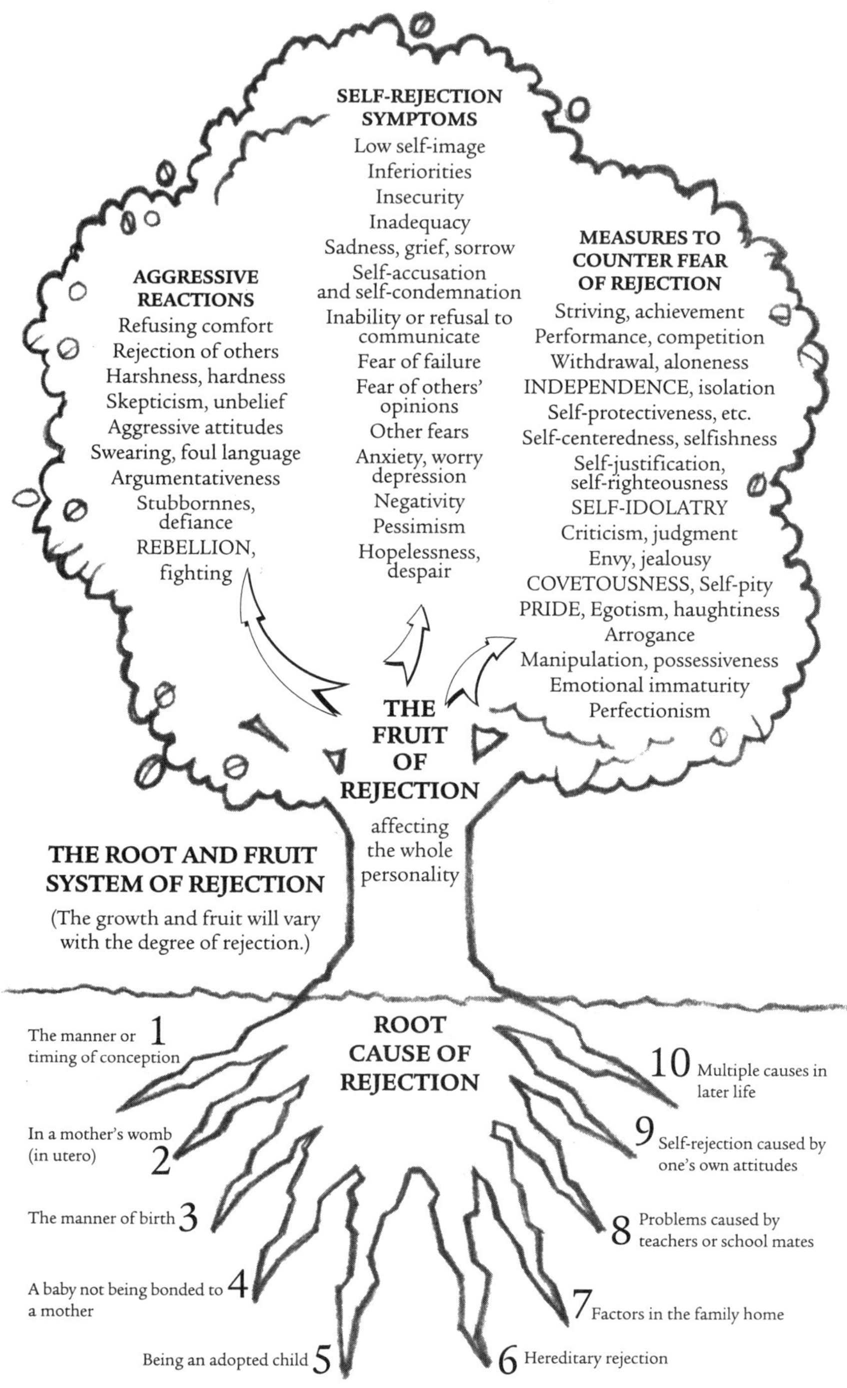

Taken from *Evicting Demonic Intruders* by Noel and Phyl Gibson (Ventura, CA: Renew Books, 1998), p.99. Used by permission.

comes to you troubled by aggressive reactions, symptoms of self-rejection, or self-centered problems, these are usually traced back to rejection in one form or another. The Gibsons taught a methodology for deliverance that they termed "whole personality deliverance." When something nasty turns up as a fruit, it can generally be traced to a root.

Let me quickly take a look at these roots and explain them a bit.

1. *Inconvenient Time*

   It could be said, "Life begins at a very early age!" The manner or timing of conception can affect a person's personality for the rest of his or her life. If the child was conceived out of wedlock or "at an inconvenient time" or was an unwanted child, a feeling of rejection will often settle in on that child for life. So, once again, work backward, and if there are evidences of rejection, seek out the cause. I always have the person pray to forgive their parents for not wanting them, and thank God that He doesn't make mistakes. I always assure the person that God wanted them to be born when and where they were born and in their particular family.

2. *Messages of Rejection in the Womb*

   Somehow, the unborn child gets messages of rejection when the mom verbalizes that she doesn't want this child or expresses the wish that she were not pregnant. If the mother is a battered wife, the child can feel "to blame," and severe feelings of rejection can result. If the person was told that he or she was unwanted at first, this could make room for a feeling of profound rejection. Happily, in many cases, parents convey to their children that it was God's will for them to have come at the time they did, and genuine love replaced the fleeting disappointment. If this is the only clue to a feeling of rejection, the person may need to forgive his or her parents for an initial disappointment and for saying something like: "I wish we weren't going to have this baby."

3. *The Manner of Birth*
   Rejection symptoms can sometimes be traced to the birth of a baby after a long and difficult labor or with the use of instruments. Occasionally a baby has suffered some birth injury or was born by Caesarian section without the benefit of a normal birth. As the Lord leads, it may be desirable to have the person pray and thank God that He did spare his or her life. The counselor may then need to rebuke the feelings of rejection from the enemy and tell them to leave in Jesus' name.

4. *Lack of Physical Bonding with the Mother*
   Babies need to be held, cuddled, stroked and generally made welcome. This is one reason why nursing is a very important part of babyhood. When some medical emergency deprives the baby of being held or if the mother simply chooses not to nurse her child, the baby is denied the bonding process and can, as a result, feel rejected. I have read sad stories about Eastern European children being kept in orphanages for long periods of time who were touched or handled only enough to care for their basic needs. These kids, even when adopted, were incapable of bonding to anyone. They had what was termed an "attachment disorder"

and could not adapt socially or in a family. They usually had rebellious and unpredictable behavior that was often destructive in nature. An absence of bonding can lead to an entry point for spirits of abandonment, isolation and loneliness that need to be expelled.

5. *Being an Adopted Child*

   Adopted children often feel rejection because the question that bothers them so deeply is, Why didn't my parents want me? I have talked to many heartbroken parents of an adopted child who are so hurt by the rebellious and uncontrollable actions of that child that they are at wits' end. Doesn't it seem strange that an adopted child, instead of being grateful to the ones who chose him or her, so often causes grief, sorrow and spiteful hurt? Strange, but it is very often the case. Spirits of abandonment are almost always present, and the rejection tree needs to be studied for any of the bad fruit that often accompanies an adoptive situation.

6. *Hereditary Rejection*

   We discussed this rather thoroughly in the last chapter, so I will just remind you that rejected people will usually reject those around them, especially the members of their own family.

7. *Factors in the Family Home*

   These problems could be myriad. When interviewing the person showing signs of rejection, we ask what special problems he or she encountered in the home during childhood. We are trying to discover "where it hurts." Some of the most common factors are an absentee father or mother; competition with siblings; verbal, sexual, or emotional abuse; constant criticism; control; alcoholism; shame of a family member; constant fighting; disinterest in the child's activities; incest; unjust discipline; being left alone because of parents' work or social activities; and so on. Usually there needs to be forgiveness extended to those who caused the felt hurt and rejection.

8. *Problems Caused by Teachers or Schoolmates*
   Let me give you a couple of examples. I frequently hear cases of children who were accused of something they did not do, and no amount of denying will convince the teacher or some schoolmate that there was a false accusation. It can be emotionally devastating to a kid when both the teacher and classmates are convinced of a false accusation.

   I was praying for a man once who told me of a severe embarrassment he suffered in the third grade. When he was a boy, he had a problem with bladder control. When he felt as though he had to go to the bathroom, he really needed to get there in a hurry. On one occasion, he raised his hand; but the teacher refused to allow him to leave the room, which resulted in an accident. The teacher brought him up in front of the class and said to the others, "Look what Billy did." He was emotionally scarred for years and had terrible nicknames, to say nothing of being excluded from activities by his classmates. Children can be very cruel. Now, if Billy were my child, I would have marched up to that teacher and demanded an apology both to Billy and the class for being cruel and rude. If I didn't get satisfaction,

I would certainly report the case to the principal. I would do everything in my power to help Billy feel he had an advocate in a difficult, frustrating situation. A teacher who is that heartless should find employment in a place other than a classroom, in my opinion.

Once again, these demons of unforgiveness, trauma and rejection can be evicted once forgiveness has been extended to the guilty parties.

9. *Self-Rejection Caused by One's Own Attitudes*
   Guilt and shame are examples of self-rejection. This is a common scar caused by having an abortion and being unable to forgive oneself. Being discontent with one's own looks, gender or some physical defect could be other examples. Confession of sin and forgiveness of oneself are usually called for before the demon of self-rejection can be cast out.

10. *Painful Factors Later in Life*
    Probably the most devastating causes are divorce, death of a spouse or unfaithfulness by a spouse. Other causes could be a broken engagement, the loss of happy employment, betrayal by a friend, broken family relationships, becoming crippled in an accident, marital incompatibility, being unable to resolve emotional problems such as depression and so on.

fruit on the rejection tree

Usually one or more of these 10 roots will produce fruit that is grouped in one or more of three sections on the branches of the rejection tree. Again, I am borrowing from Noel and Phyl Gibson when I make these lists, because I have found none better or more complete.

Aggressive Reactions

Often, rebellion is a major symptom of aggressive feelings. As a matter of fact, I often use the phrase "rejection breeds rebellion." (I am sorry to say that I have used it so much that I honestly can't remember if it is original or I borrowed it from some other person! I am now pleading my being close to 70 years of age as a reason for lapses like this.) Others in the aggressive reaction cluster are refusing comfort, rejection of others, harshness, hardness, skepticism, unbelief, aggressive attitudes, swearing, foul language, arguing, stubbornness, defiance and fighting. A sentence that would describe the behavior of the person who possesses these symptoms would sound something like this: "If somebody didn't want me, I'll show them!"

Self-Rejection Symptoms

These symptoms include a low self-image; feelings of inferiority; insecurity and inadequacy; sadness; grief and sorrow; self-accusation and self-condemnation; inability or refusal to communicate; fear of all sorts (especially fear of failure and the opinions of other people); anxiety, worry, depression, negativity, pessimism, hopelessness and despair. To this list I would add self-punishment and eating disorders. Someone displaying a number of these symptoms might say or think: "They said they didn't want me and they were right; I'm not worth anything at all."

> *Measures to Counter Fear of Rejection*
> These are listed as striving, achievement, performance, competition, withdrawal, aloneness, independence, isolation, self-protectiveness, self-centeredness, selfishness, self-justification, self-righteousness, self-idolatry, criticism (or a critical spirit), judgment, envy, jealousy, covetousness, self-pity, pride, egotism, haughtiness, arrogance, manipulation and control, possessiveness, emotional immaturity and perfectionism. A person suffering in this way might say: "Somebody didn't want me; I'll prove that *I am somebody!*"

Once again, we work backward from the symptoms to the entry point. The fruit will lead to the root. Demons of rejection that have gained entry are common and often costly to a person. When a person requests prayer for deliverance, more often than not rejection needs to be investigated.

Remember, I mentioned once before that when rejection is present, always look for three other sorts of subspirits that frequently accompany it. These are inherited rejection (which I have explained), perceived rejection and fear of rejection. I usually pray against all four because they frequently turn up in this pattern.

demons are liars

A demon bringing *perceived rejection* is a big, fat liar. It tells its host that rejection is present when it really is not. It's as though a filter was placed on the mind of the person and many innocent statements are consequently interpreted as statements or inferences of rejection. If something can be interpreted as positive or negative, the negative interpretation will automatically be accepted as truth, even though it was the farthest thing from the mind of the one who said it. Persons suffering from rejection usually have perceived rejection to some degree. Unless there is a broken relationship caused by some misinterpreted perceived rejection needing forgiveness, I usually just kick this one out.

Fear of rejection robs a person of joy. He or she is constantly on guard against what other people may think. Such a person wrestles with thoughts like, *I can't do that* or *What will they think if I wear that?* And the list goes on and on. The basic problem here is that the person needs acceptance, a feeling of belonging, and Satan wants to steal it. So be sure to pray against a spirit of the fear of rejection along with those mentioned above. I frequently pray for a blessing of confidence to replace it.

receiving the love of God

I sometimes need to spend some time after praying over rejection in all its forms by reassuring these people about God's love for them. With the fatherlessness of this generation, or having had an abusive father, some people can't think of God the Father as a God of love. They need to hear things like: "God didn't make a mistake when He made you"; "God loved the world (and He had you in mind when He made that statement) so much that He sent Jesus to die for you—He would have done it if you were the only one in the world"; "God did not approve of the unjust beatings you got as a kid—He felt your pain and He understands your feelings, but let's ask God to take them away." To recap, I usually pray to expel the three subspirits of rejection and then go for the major spirit of rejection last.

I always pray healing over the memories of a person who has been rejected or abused. I ask God to take away the sting so that if a particularly painful memory comes to mind again, the hurt will be healed and gone. We ask the Holy Spirit to fill the places with His presence where there were formerly memories of hurt. I remind the person that forgiveness has been extended to the one who was guilty, and if the devil tries to incite unforgiveness again, it should not be difficult to resist.

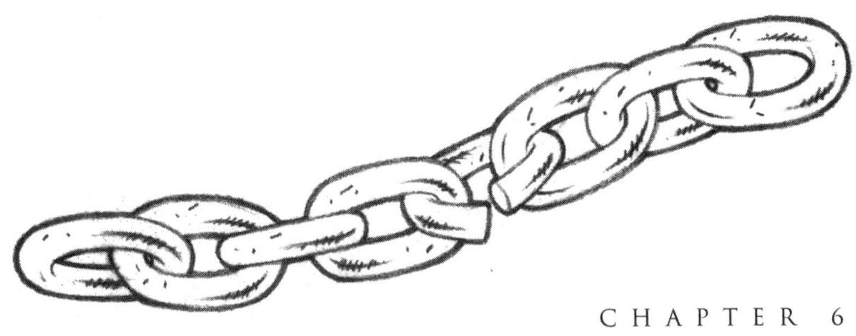

CHAPTER 6

victimization

molestation, rape and sexual exploitation

I hate to see the devil pick on kids or helpless people. It's just not fair. But then, who says the devil plays by decent rules? We need to realize the awful cruelty of our enemy.

when children are targets

Of all of the ways that the devil abuses human beings, victimizing children is about the sickest and the effects can be felt throughout life. Let me give you an example and try to explain it from my experience. I remind you once again that I am not a psychologist or professional counselor. I am just a mom and grandma who has lived a long time and learned a few things along the way.

A defunct news service called the *National and International Religion Report* carried this story on December 13, 1993, from which I will take excerpts:

> In one of the worst criminal cases of pedophilia in the United States, former Catholic priest James Porter was sentenced to 18-20 years in prison for the molestation of dozens of boys and girls in three eastern Massachusetts parishes in the 1960s. He could be considered for parole in about six years.
>
> Porter, 58, overpowered or ambushed his victims, often telling them they would be punished if they told anyone of the incidents. Prior to sentencing, Porter listened to a litany of charges from the adults he had assaulted as children. In court they told anguished stories of their assaults, shattered childhoods, and hopes for vindication.
>
> At least half of the 22 victims who testified were speaking publicly for the first time. Several bitterly denounced the failure of the Catholic Church to act promptly, even when some parents told church officials that Porter had sexually assaulted their children. *Victims described themselves as being plagued by nightmares, depression, drug and alcohol addictions, suicide attempts, and failed marriages* (author's emphasis).
>
> Porter admitted to molesting nearly 100 children in Massachusetts, but victim advocates say he may have abused more.

On Sunday, December 12, 1993, the *Rocky Mountain News* carried on page 22 a short report of the same story with a slightly different twist. Let me quote that for you:

> PRIEST SENTENCED IN MOLESTATIONS
> In New Bedford, Mass., former priest James Porter was sentenced Monday to at least 18 years in prison for child

molesting after 22 of his victims spoke of the pain and embarrassment they quietly endured for three decades.

Before the sentence was announced, Porter tearfully begged for leniency, but one victim told the judge: "I would ask the court to show the same amount of mercy that Mr. Porter showed us, and that is none." Prosecutors had urged up to 40 years in jail.

The former Roman Catholic priest pleaded guilty October 5 to 27 charges of indecent assault and battery of a child under 14, as well as 14 related charges. *Porter admitted he was still a pedophile* (author's emphasis).

teenage mothers

It was very interesting to me that on that same page of the *Rocky Mountain News* another much more prominent story was printed. The story was probably more prominent, I concluded, because it was a story by Bill Scanlon, a news staff writer for the paper, and the story was about Denver. A large headline read: TEENAGE MOTHERS OFTEN HAVE HISTORY OF VICTIMIZATION. A slightly less prominent subheader stated: "Many of Denver's young moms abused before they became pregnant, public school officials report." Here is what the article said:

> Most of Denver's teenage mothers were physically or sexually abused long before they became pregnant, the director of the Denver public school for teen mothers says.
>
> "Sexuality was something that was forced on them," said Sally Hodson, principal of Florence Crittenton School in west Denver.
>
> "Their relationship with other people, particularly

males, is one of victimization. They gravitate toward violent boyfriends who beat them up."

In the poverty-stricken neighborhoods making up almost half of Denver, there are four births for every five girls during their teen years according to the latest statistics.

Children born to teen mothers are several times more likely than other youngsters to grow up in poverty, to live in a fatherless home, and to fall into the cycle of crime, unemployment, and poor education.

Rarely did these girls go home from school to a stable family, Hodson said. "They don't go home to a mom and dad. They go home to drug and alcohol abuse and drug dealing. Poverty doesn't help.

"We're dealing with the aftereffects of people manipulating and abusing them," Hodson said (author's emphasis).

A 1991 survey of 500 teen mothers in Seattle found that 66% had been fondled, molested, or raped at some time in their lives. Hodson said the rate of molestation or abuse among the teens at Crittenton is "the same or higher" than the Seattle study.

"Some are very reluctant to talk about it and don't mention it until counselors speak to them at length," she said.

Officials said they could see the effects of abuse. "We see it in their behavior. They deal with the world as victims. They don't have the realization that they can tell other people it's not OK to be victimized."

The Seattle study found that teenage mothers who had been abused were more likely to have used drugs, suffered poor self-esteem, and been unable to bond with their babies.

Probably the first emotion you felt when you read this was one of sadness for these poor victimized youngsters whose lives have been so scarred. Some will never recover, and once again we can see how the devil steals, kills and destroys. It is a tragedy.

This chapter will deal with the demonic entry points of predators who go around victimizing people, how the victimized suffer demonic infestation, pass it on to others and how the cycle perpetuates unless there is spiritual intervention. That spiritual intervention is what I hope to convey so that we can take back some of what the devil has stolen.

there is hope all around

But the message we must convey now is that there is hope for spiritual repair for both the victim and perpetrator alike. We do not condone the sin or crime at all, and the guilty must pay the debt owed to society. As a matter of fact, being soft on crime or criminals has been at the root of much of today's societal struggles, in my opinion. Even Jesus didn't make arrangements to take the repentant thief down from his cross; He only pardoned the thief and told him that he would be with Him later on that same day in paradise.

California had gained somewhat of a reputation for its liberality when it came to crime and certain social issues during the time we lived there in the '70s and '80s. We voters had to check the ballots over carefully each Election Day. One day while living there, I heard over the radio that a judge had dismissed a case involving the rape of a 12-year-old girl, as I recall. The judge said that the girl, who didn't get pregnant, wasn't hurt, so the case was dismissed. I'm sorry I can't document this, but it was quite typical of a sad judicial system that was soft on crime. This was quite common back in the early '80s. No mention was made in that case of emotional damage to the girl, and there may have been more to the story than was broadcast, but it left the listener with the impression that rape is okay as long as the female doesn't become pregnant.

too many loopholes

My question concerning Mr. Porter is, why weren't charges pressed when the church failed to act? I am not sure when the rule came into effect, but counselors now know that they must report cases of child molestation to the authorities to get child predators identified. There still seem to be loopholes, however, and all too many dangerous people are on the loose. As with Mr. Porter, if the demon is not expelled, the person will remain afflicted and is very likely to commit the crime again.

If a child claims to have been raped, it is a serious matter. In days gone by, children were threatened, as Mr. Porter did with his victims, and many kept quiet out of fear. Sad to say, many weren't believed, and stories were dismissed as wild fantasy. Little by little, however, society is waking up. These things are investigated more readily now than in days past when even talking about these actions was unheard of. The well-being of our children comes first, and every measure possible must be taken to lock up these child predators.

Jesus had some very strong words to say about those who offend little ones. In Luke 17:1,2 He says, "It is impossible that no offenses should come, but woe *to him* through whom they do come! It would be better for him if a millstone were hung around his neck, and he were thrown into the sea, than that he should offend one of these little ones." We could interpret this to mean that leading a child astray or offending a child is indeed a very serious matter. I don't think we stretch the meaning of the text too much to believe that it could mean sexually abusing a child.

asking the right questions

James Porter admitted to the crimes and also admitted to still being a pedophile at the time of his sentencing. Deliverance workers agree that pedophilia is demonic in nature. If Mr. Porter had called and asked for prayer, how would we begin to interview him? Several obvious questions come to mind. Was he raped as a child? Was there incest in his family? Did his first desires to commit rape against a child appear after having been involved with kiddy porn? Was he conceived out of wedlock? (Children conceived in lust often struggle with lust.)

I would also ask the usual questions concerning sexual problems. Some of those questions are, Is compulsive masturbation a problem? Does pornography have a hold on his life? Has he had problems with fornication, bestiality, prostitutes, sexual fantasy and the like? We will thoroughly discuss these in the chapter on sexual demons, but here we gather information and diagnose when the problem began.

Notice I mention in the paragraph above, "If Mr. Porter...asked for prayer." A person must *want* to get rid of the afflicting demons for deliverance to be effective and long lasting. As strange as it may seem, some people are very comfortable with demons in their lives and choose not to give them up. We cannot make that choice for them. One of the first rules for a successful deliverance is that the person must want to be free. But if Mr. Porter said he did want ministry, I would head off to jail to visit him with the permission of the authorities.

I would first of all look into Mr. Porter's spiritual condition and see if he has ever asked Jesus to be his personal savior. I would then explain the way of salvation and ask him to receive Christ if he has not done it before. If he has, I would proceed from there.

closing entry points one at a time

In the case of Mr. Porter, after analyzing what we would call the entry points, each of those would need to be dealt with, one at a time. He would need to forgive anyone who raped him. He would need to forgive anyone who introduced him to kiddy porn and beg help for them and mercy on their souls. And so on.

He would need to ask God's forgiveness for his sexual sins and crimes. Then, one by one, I would expel the demons by the same name, such as pornography, compulsive masturbation, sexual fantasy and especially pedophilia. Of course I would need to collect many bits of information concerning his history, and I would quite likely find things such as rejection and victimization from which he had suffered. I would then command the demons to leave, one by one, in the name of Jesus.

Sexual sins are almost always accompanied by spirits of guilt and shame. These need to be ordered out also. We would most likely discover that Mr. Porter really didn't ever want to act this way and that it was something totally beyond his control. Here, when we are pretty certain that he has Christ in his heart, we need to assure him that God is capable of forgiving all his sin. The guilt and shame may have been so bad that he thought he was beyond the point of forgiveness. We find this every now and then. If this is the case, he might need to pray for two more things: to forgive himself and to forgive God.

That sounds strange, I know, but as we interview people all sorts of strange things often come out. He may blame God for not stopping him from harming these kids, even though his will was overriding God's will. Some people habitually seek to blame anyone or anything instead of themselves. So it would be necessary to find out what Mr. Porter's feelings were on this and then pray accordingly.

mending fences

Mr. Porter would have some major fence mending to do after we are sure we have prayed through everything and have asked the Holy Spirit to cleanse him and fill him completely. As God would lead, I might suggest some of the following: He would need to apologize to kids, families, churches, communities and anyone else he felt God would require. He would need to pay his debt to society. He would need to confess to the proper authorities and to all others involved anything the state hasn't convicted him of constituting a felony or misdemeanor. He would need to pray for the spiritual, physical and emotional healing of everyone he offended. And he would have to do anything else God might require.

praying for the victims

Let's say that one of Mr. Porter's victims—we'll call her Suzie Q.—comes and asks for prayer. She is a victim who suffers from depression and a failed marriage. How would we go about praying for her? Let's read a paragraph from *Evicting Demonic Intruders* by Noel and Phyl Gibson (Renew Books) to help us look for some specifics. I quote from page 191:

> *Sexual Problems Caused by Molestation, Incest or Rape*
> These experiences are usually totally devastating and cause both immediate and long-term problems. The sense of defilement the victims suffer will often make them withdraw and become emotionally cold. Long-term results may include sexual frigidity in marriage. Others become lustful, masturbate and indulge in promiscuity as they have convinced themselves that no decent person would be attracted to them. Deliverance, cleansing and renewal are essential for them to regain self-respect and a healthy attitude to sex and marriage.

As I have worked with so many victimized persons over the years, I have discovered some additional emotional problems that seem to pop up frequently. These include, but are probably not limited to, demons of trauma, anger, violence, unforgiveness, bitterness, hatred, a man-hating spirit, prostitution, pornography and many other lustful habits, fears, rage and others. Emotions that need healing often include various symptoms of rejection and anger toward God.

> Let's say that Suzie Q. became a Christian some years ago, but she now realizes she needs healing from the experiences she suffered at the hand of Mr. Porter. I would investigate her background and list her hurtful symptoms. I would deal with all inherited items first and then go on to ask her to forgive Mr. Porter. I would deal

with each problem one at a time, expelling every demon that has been tormenting her.

inner healing

Suzie Q. would need a long prayer for inner healing. I would pray cleansing over each area of her body that was defiled. I would break a soul-tie with Mr. Porter and any other person with whom she has had illicit sexual activity. In cases of sexual sins or victimization, I always pray healing over the five senses, the memory and the emotions. I ask God to heal the trauma and pictures seared in their minds or memories. I always pray cleansing over their brain, skin, hands, feet and sexual organs, as well as anything inappropriate that they have seen, heard, touched, smelled or tasted.

breaking soul-ties

How do we break a soul-tie, and why do they need breaking in the first place? Another favorite book of mine is *Healing Through Deliverance 2: The Practical Ministry* by Peter Horrobin (Ventura, CA: Renew Books, 1995). His explanation and discussion of soul-ties is very helpful. He says on page 81:

> The demonic can transfer to the victim directly from the perpetrator of violence through the ungodly soul-tie which is created through the attack, or through the fear which is a natural consequence of being attacked in this way.

On page 238, Mr. Horrobin goes on to give a very helpful sample prayer on how to break a soul-tie:

PRAYER:

In the name of the Father, the Son, and the Holy Spirit, I break all ungodly spirit, soul, and body ties that have been established between you and (speak out here the name of the individual involved). *I sever that linking supernaturally and ask God to remove from you all influence of the other person* (name the person again here if you prefer), *and draw back to yourself every part which has been wrongfully tied in bondage to another person* (again name the person here if you prefer).

This prayerful statement may then be followed up by a prayer for deliverance of any demons that entered through the particular soul-ties being referred to at each stage. If you are ready to move straight on to deliverance, continue as follows:

I now speak directly to every evil spirit that has taken advantage of this ungodly soul-tie. You no longer have any rights here, and I order you to leave now without hurting or harming (name here the individual being prayed for), *or any other person, and without going into any other member of the family. In Jesus' name. Amen.*

You would do well to keep these prayers handy. When you pray for a person who has been victimized by someone who is not his or her spouse or has created an ungodly soul-tie, these prayers can serve as models. In very simple terms, a soul-tie can serve as a highway to transport demons from the perpetrator to the victim. It is a bit of a mystery to me how all this junk can enter, but if any of the spirits plaguing a victim come to mind when praying about the soul-tie, order them out. I usually pray in a manner very similar as Peter Horrobin and simply address *every* evil spirit that has taken advantage of the soul-tie.

breaking the cycle

Carefully review the section about Denver's and Seattle's teenage mothers who were physically or sexually abused. You will note that they were victims. Some gravitated toward violent boyfriends. It could be that as they were being victimized, a spirit of violence transferred onto them, as well as evil sexual demons that encouraged them to lead a life of sin, further victimization or trauma. And the cycle is quite likely to continue in their offspring.

The explanation that poor education, poverty and other social problems are the cause is not entirely accurate, in my opinion. We find more of these problems in places that have these three symptoms, because once the problems of victimization occur, a sort of infestation takes place and demons are multiplied. In my opinion, demonic activity is often the cause of the social problems so prevalent in certain areas. The social situation may in fact be the *effect* of demonic activity, not the *cause* of the problems we so often see in the inner city. Social help, welfare and education are only part of the assistance needed. Real and lasting change will come from removing root causes in the lives of individuals.

When Christ declared that He was sent "to set at liberty those who are oppressed" (Luke 4:18), undoubtedly, He had places like our current-day slums, inner cities and other major territorial demonic strongholds in mind. If those called to minister to the oppressed are not equipped to cast out demons, they have one hand tied behind their backs and will never be as effective as God wants them to be. Add this ingredient to social assistance, education and training, and major changes for the better will undoubtedly be accelerated.

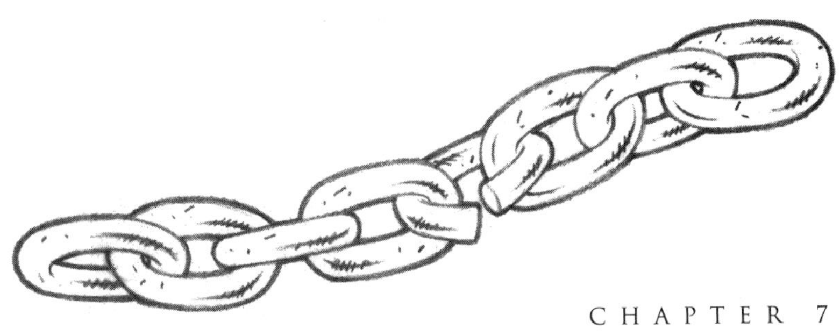

CHAPTER 7

occult practices

witchcraft, freemasonry and deliberate sin

When we speak about the probability of demonic entry through experiences of the occult, satanism, witchcraft and Freemasonry, we could really have a one-word chapter called "Yes."

idolatry is worse than some think

When individuals expose themselves to these forms of worship and activity, they are worshiping demons, and the power by which they operate is demonic in nature. It ties in somewhat with idolatry and the first two commandments: "I am the Lord your God.... You shall have no other gods before Me. You shall not make for yourself a carved image—any likeness *of anything*...you shall not bow down to them nor serve them" (Exod. 20:2-5). As one of our daughters said when she was a little girl, "Idolatry makes God really mad." Many adults should be as perceptive.

God gave clear instructions in the Law to the children of Israel when he said in Leviticus 19:26 *(NIV)*, "Do not practice divination or sorcery." He went on to say in Leviticus 19:31 *(NIV)*, "Do not turn to mediums or seek out spiritists, for you will be defiled by them. I am the LORD your God." In the next chapter, Leviticus 20:6 *(NIV)* says, "I will set my face against the person who turns to mediums and spiritists to prostitute himself by following them, and I will cut him off from his people."

Deuteronomy 18 gives further strong teaching, but probably the strongest is in Deuteronomy 17:2-5 (*NIV*). This passage says, "If a man or a woman...is found doing evil in the eyes of the LORD your God in violation of his covenant, and contrary to my command has worshiped other gods, bowing down to them or to the sun or the moon or the stars of the sky...if it is true and has been proved that this detestable thing has been done in Israel, take the man or woman who has done this evil deed to your city gate and stone that person to death."

Choosing to worship and/or serve any spiritual being other than Jehovah God is absolutely wrong and is invariably an entry point for demons. When Satan is worshiped, the evil spirits that gain entry are particularly strong and put up an inevitable fight upon being evicted.

God warned His people over and over in Old Testament times to totally forsake witchcraft, sorcery, divination and idolatry. Somehow it seemed to draw them irresistibly. When witchcraft has been practiced in a family, it can become an inherited problem, as I mentioned before. Children are usually indoctrinated into the system when they are young and continue in the practice. The family has made covenant with the kingdom of darkness, and the curses can follow on down the family line.

On the other hand, when godly parents make covenant with God, they have made it with the kingdom of light, and the blessings follow down their family line. Willful disobedience, sin and deliberate acts of witchcraft or satanic activity can cause a rift in the flow of blessing. This is contrary to the will of God and is a major cause of demonization.

The two books that I highly recommend and ask my students to read are *Evicting Demonic Intruders* by Noel and Phyl Gibson (Ventura, CA: Renew Books, 1993) and *Healing Through Deliverance 2: The Practical Ministry* by Peter Horrobin (Ventura, CA: Renew Books, 1995). These have very complete discussions of occultism and witchcraft accompanied by extensive and helpful glossaries of terms explaining what we face in the deliverance of someone coming out of the occult. Do take advantage of these authors' vast knowledge and experience in this field by reading both of these books before attempting to deal with someone who has this background. They will give you excellent help and background on breaking curses that accompany witchcraft, the occult and satanism.

freemasonry

Noel Gibson's chapter on Freemasonry is a classic. He gave me permission to copy it and hand it out in my seminars in the past, but I now recommend getting his whole book. However, the chapter title will give you a hint of its contents: "Freemasons Curse Themselves, Their Families and Their Churches." Let me briefly summarize what he says about Freemasonry, excerpting from page 132.

> Freemasonry rightly claims to be a religion. Lodges are "holy ground." Worship and prayers are to a divine person...but its central deity is anti-God and anti-Christ.

> The central deity...is an object of satanic syncretism in which the Jehovah of the Bible is blasphemously linked with mythological demonic deities. Worship is therefore idolatrous and brings Freemasons directly under the curse of God.
>
> Holders of the highest degrees in Freemasonry are committed to the belief that Lucifer alone is God. They exalt the one whom God has thrown out of His presence and for whom the lake of fire has been prepared as eternal punishment.
>
> Freemasons who profess to be Christian cause the curse of God to fall also upon their families and their churches because of their gross and blasphemous idolatry.
>
> Demonic bondages and dominations in families of Lodge members emphasizes the great need for the visible Church to be cleansed from all Freemason associations, and all family members delivered from demonic oppression.

God has provided for us the best tool I have ever seen to help Freemasons and their descendants break the curses and get themselves out of the bondages from which they suffer. Selwyn Stevens, a brother from New Zealand, has produced a prayer in his book *Unmasking Freemasonry—Removing the Hoodwink* (Wellington, New Zealand: Jubilee Resources, 1999). He encourages copying the prayer, provided proper reference is made. I have prepared this prayer in its entirety in appendix 5 of this book. Information on how to order his book is there also.

I received word that since Brother Selwyn began circulating this prayer and informing the public and the church in New Zealand about the reality of Freemasonry, over 20 percent of the Freemasons in New Zealand have requested to have their names removed from the rolls in the last four years. Education, in this case, is a very helpful thing.

deliberate sin

So far, much of the discussion in this book has pointed out how Satan takes advantage of individuals to create bondages, some of which a person inherited, with others resulting from being victimized. But very often bad choices or deliberate rebellion against good teaching or against God Himself may also throw a door wide open for a demon to enter.

God carefully wrote out the Ten Commandments and gave them to Moses for the children of Israel. When the tablets of stone were broken, He kindly gave them to Moses a second time so that this basic set of rules could be preserved in the hearts of all until they became part of the Jewish culture. This is history. But even in Scripture they appear twice, once in Exodus 20 and again in Deuteronomy 5, because of their great importance. God really meant what He said! Chapter 5 of Deuteronomy concludes with several verses promising blessing to the people if they would obey the commandments. Verse 29 says, in part (and this is Moses quoting from the Lord Himself): "Oh, that they had such a heart in them that they would fear Me and always keep all My commandments, that it might be well with them and their children forever!" The Ten Commandments are given for our *good* so that we might live in peace and happiness.

However, people are put together in such a way that they sometimes want to see just how close to the fire they can get without being burned. People facetiously say, "Rules were made to be broken."

Peter and I raised three wonderful girls, but they weren't born wonderful. They had to be taught, corrected, encouraged and taught again. After they left home, we could only pray that they had been taught and corrected enough to have established healthy patterns that would automatically lead them to right choices most of the time. To teach children obedience is a great favor to them. Our girls and their husbands love the Lord. They are our friends and they are a great joy to us. And they, in turn, are teaching their kids well, but the job has become more difficult for them because of the changes in American society that I have mentioned.

Disobedience to biblical teaching is dangerous. Some disadvantaged people haven't had the Bible taught to them. They sin out of ignorance. But those who know better, and in spite of that knowledge either yield to temptation or invite sin into their lives, often open a door to demons.

Some of the more common openings to spirits that can enslave a person start out with self-indulgences that can easily become addictions. We have discussed these previously, but let's list a few of the more common ones again: nicotine, drugs, alcohol, gambling, overeating, overexercising and being a spendthrift. Certain sexual problems are also highly addictive, such as compulsive masturbation and pornography.

glorifying the creature, not the Creator

Leaving the worship of God to investigate eastern religions and later start to join in some of their ceremonies can be a willful disobedience that may prove costly indeed. It is idolatry, pure and simple, and once again, "Idolatry really makes God mad." When pagan statues are brought into a person's home, demonic spirits may come along with them and cause strange and unidentifiable problems within the person's four walls.

For example, pagan statues (such as mythical gods and goddesses); carved images of any creature or person known to be worshiped in any part of the world; photos, paintings or artifacts such as totem poles have no place in a Christian's home. Many of these are passed off as "native art" and have actually been used in pagan worship ceremonies. Do not be deceived into thinking that these things have no power. They can carry demons attached to them that can change the spiritual atmosphere of your home drastically. Just because you are a committed Christian does not mean you are immune to demonic harassment if you bring one home with you.

If you are rooming with another person and that individual has something that glorifies "the creature rather than the Creator" (Rom. 1:25), I would talk about it with that person and ask to have it removed. If the person refuses to do so, at least pray over the item and bind any spirits attached to it, asking God to render them helpless in your home. If the item is not yours, you have no authority to remove or destroy it. You can pray, however, that your roommate will remove the item soon.

Another major entry point so easy to fall into in this day and age is just plain inviting demons in by befriending them through demonic video games and demonic music with lyrics suggesting death, suicide, vile behavior, disobedience and all types of filth and violence.

magnets for lust

Sexual activity outside of marriage and habits of pornography, compulsive masturbation, homosexual behavior, bestiality, pedophilia and other lustful activities are major openings for demons to take over and ruin the kind of life that God intended. The mind becomes so polluted that good thoughts just don't stay there very long. Pornography is highly addictive and contaminating to the mind and, strangely enough, many pastors and other Christian leaders are stuck in this private addiction. They become ineffective in their ministry because of this distraction. The guilt and shame that accompany this vile addiction overcome them with grief at times.

I have heard of so many cases of porn in the lives of pastors that you wonder how they ever got involved in the first place. Many have picked up a plain old spirit of lust from watching something X-rated in a hotel one night when they were away from home. Of course, instead of "fleeing youthful lust," they like to believe they are "doing a sociological investigation." It only takes one anopheles mosquito bite to infect a person with a lifelong case of malaria. A demon of lust could attach itself to them through something as simple as one bad movie, and it is downhill from there until they get help.

Another way lust enters a pastor's mind is through innocent counseling. Sometimes the woman who has asked for counseling, usually marital counseling, is a witch with a deliberate assignment to cast a lustful spell on the pastor in order to harm his ministry, marriage or parish. Sometimes it is simply an imprudent woman who might fall into the "dingbat" category. Typically, she dresses provocatively and demonstrates little culture or good taste. She may discuss her sexual or marriage problems with graphic details, and lustful thoughts can invade the pastor's mind. A little later on he buys his first "soft-porn" magazine and soon is hopelessly hooked.

I always counsel classes of pastors whom I am teaching to give female marital-counseling cases to a female counselor or intercessor who can at least pray for the woman first. A woman is quite unlikely to divulge graphic sexual details to another woman; a handsome young pastor is a much more likely candidate, or so advises the lustful spirit inside of her. If all else fails, a mature woman should be invited to join the counseling session to keep a lid on things. The mature woman can take copious notes for the pastor that might help modify the sexual minutiae expressed by the female counselee.

Another sad entry point for a spirit of lust in men is the wife's withholding sex from her husband as punishment for him or as a weapon of some sort for personal gain. If it becomes an undesirable pattern, the husband might seek sex elsewhere, starting with an "adult" channel on his TV after hours, some pornographic literature to satisfy his fantasy lust, taking a quick peek on the Internet or resorting to masturbation or even an affair.

Wives, be warned, and learn from this. Sex is not a weapon. Never withhold sex from your husband. He understands occasional illness, female cycles, surgery and the like; but this is by mutual consent and understanding, and only very occasionally or temporarily. If sex is not enjoyable, check things out with your doctor or a Christian counselor. First of all, pray that God will fix things in your marriage. Men, be kind and gentle. Brutality and kinky behavior are unacceptable in a Christian marriage. If things don't get resolved, it would be safe to assume that there may be some demons at work, and the next step would be to get some deliverance. I am convinced that God gave sex within marriage to be thoroughly enjoyed by both partners.

Willful disobedience to God's rules and regulations for Christian behavior as found in Scripture can be, and often is, an opening for any kind of spirit. I can honestly say that willful disobedience is unhealthy for both the body and soul.

holiness and prayer

Nothing can take the place of a life of holiness and prayer. Keeping close to God, daily Bible reading, listening to worship music when able, and teaming up with prayer partners to pray for one another, are all ways God has given us to avoid sin. I'm sure each believer eventually wants to hear, "Well done, *good and faithful servant*" (Matt. 25:21,23, emphasis added).

We can't plead ignorance. That's why we have the Bible and churches. Learn and obey the rules and pray the prayer every day, slowly and deliberately:

And forgive us our sins,
For we also forgive everyone who is indebted to us.
And do not lead us into temptation,
But deliver us from the evil one (Luke 11:4).

Demons will have a tough time penetrating this protective wall. If this is a way of life, they will get discouraged and look for a more likely candidate, believe me. Holiness is like getting an inoculation against demons. It's a sure thing.

CHAPTER 8

a deliverance session

preparation and operation

Let me share from my experience some pointers on preparing to minister deliverance to someone. I will comment on a number of items.

getting ready

You are the deliverance leader of the session. Please keep in mind that of primary importance is your own spiritual preparation and condition. Above all else, do not attempt deliverance on someone else if there are demonic footholds in your own life. Demons seem to know when the person who is counseling and praying has "critters" hanging on to him or her. That could prove embarrassing to everyone because the demons you are working to expel might just tell you so.

Therefore, you must be free from demonic presence in your own life. You must be living a pure life with no known sin lurking anywhere. That gives you a "right" to minister to the life of another person and assures you of the authority to do it in the name of Jesus.

You need to be "prayed up." Ask the Lord for His special help and guidance as you look over the questionnaire and pray for wisdom, discernment and compassion to minister effectively.

I usually fast on the day of a deliverance. As I look into the practice of other deliverance ministers, I find that some do and some don't. Those who do deliverance on a daily basis need to eat sometime. I am able to do it only occasionally at this point in my life, so fasting is a luxury I can well afford.

A feature that comes along with experience is confidence. You must be a person of faith and confidence. Your faith grows in this area until you are sure that God will come to your aid each time you pray and that he will increase your authority. The job gets easier as time goes by and as your experience mounts.

Remember our two chief weapons: the *authority* our Lord has given and the use of the *name of Jesus* as we address each demon by name, commanding it to leave.

THE SUPPORT OF INTERCESSORS

I like to have some of my intercessors know when I will be doing deliverance so they can uphold the session in prayer. If the person for whom I am praying is comfortable in asking for prayer from his or her Christian friends, that can help also. I do not divulge the name of the person I am praying for or the nature of the problems. I am very careful to maintain privacy and dignity as much as is possible. I usually just say something like, "I am praying for a woman on Tuesday at 9 A.M. and it could be a difficult case. Please pray for wisdom, discernment and the help of the Holy Spirit in great measure."

WORKING WITH A TEAM

If you are working with a small team of people, be sure that only one person is in charge of the session at a time. It is never to become a free-for-all with several people praying or speaking at a time. When I am working with a team, I ask that any suggestions that my team has be written on a piece of paper and handed to me. If I request someone to say something, that is a different story. Demons thrive on confusion because they can get a bit of an advantage in chaos. My advice is to keep things calm and in order.

TRAINING OTHERS

It is wonderful if team members can be "apprenticed" in actual deliverance sessions, but this should be done with just one or two at a time. As they are sitting in on a session, their job is to intercede. If they have questions, they are to be written down and never asked out loud during the session. Debriefing is to be done in private after the session is over.

It is also a good learning technique to have the person being apprenticed go over the questionnaire with you ahead of time. You can point out what is "as plain as the nose on your face." I usually write down the name of the demon I will be going after in the margin. I highlight in pink (you can use any color!) significant items that require either further explanation or attention in prayer.

The person being apprenticed needs to promise to maintain strict confidentiality. This must never be betrayed, even for "prayer purposes" (too many prayer meetings become gossip sessions). If you have private information and you feel it needs prayer, you are probably the person God wants to do the praying. Of course, if the person requesting deliverance asks you to have some intercessors pray, that is a different story, but we still insist on confidentiality. Generally, a person will ask for prayer if there has been involvement in witchcraft or satanism. Fear is always present in abundant supply. Seasoned intercessors usually know how to keep their lips buttoned. Those who cannot don't qualify as deliverance intercessors.

We need to assure the person requesting deliverance that to be with us is to be in a safe place where confidentiality is respected and guarded. The devil would like nothing more than to bring insecurity to the individual by having misgivings about our keeping confidence. He also enjoys embarrassing his victims. We just won't give him that satisfaction!

An interesting thing happens after I pray for an individual. Since I am naturally a rather tender person who can't stand conflict, God supernaturally removes almost all of what I pray from my mind so that I just don't remember it. If I ever had to carry the load of garbage I pray about, it would make me an emotional basket case! God is very kind, and I can meet the person I prayed for later on and look him or her straight in the eye without any "baggage" attached. I also make it a point to never converse about a past deliverance session. This may be a reason why it "evaporates" from my memory—I just don't reinforce it by talking about it.

the person requesting prayer

There are several requirements I insist upon before agreeing to pray for a person.

This does not mean I refuse to pray for that person. It usually means the person is not yet ready. When the person agrees to the following requirements, I will set up an appointment.

The person must desire to be free.
It can't be the idea of the spouse, grandfather or a friend. It must be his or her sincere desire.

The person must be willing to forgive those who have been the root causes of their problems.
This can be hard to do; but until the person is willing to forgive, prayer must be postponed, since unforgiveness can be an invitation for the problem to return.

The person must be serious about promising to stop sin, break bad habits, perhaps let go of certain friendships, or do whatever will assist in the healing process.
I am unable to hold people's hands after I pray for them. I advise them to follow the Post-Prayer Instructions (see Appendix 4) and expect them to do so in order to maintain satisfactory results and lasting freedom.

The person must promise to keep close to God.
A steady diet of regular church attendance, daily Bible reading and prayer will be expected. Small-group attendance is desirable, when available, to assist in accountability.

the physical place of prayer

I always insist on being in a safe place for prayer. If I need to pray alone for a man, I do it in my office. There are windows with no shades, and I pray during business hours only. I was fortunate enough to design my own office, and from my desk I can see through windows to the right and left of me. I can see everyone in a straight line through these windows. This protects us all, and we cannot be accused of "being behind a closed door." Even our conference rooms have large floor-to-ceiling windows so that any passerby can see when the room is occupied.

I always place my chair directly opposite the person for whom I am praying. In this way I can look straight into his or her eyes. I am certain my guest is not looking into the sunshine or the bright light of a window. I always provide a glass of water, a box of tissues and a wastebasket within handy reach of us both. If there are any other persons present, they sit off to one side of me, easily within arm's reach in case they need to discreetly hand me a note.

I push the "do not disturb" button on my phone and hang a "do not disturb" sign on my door. I convey to my guest that I am giving my undivided attention to the matters at hand.

gathering further information

I would have received the confidential questionnaire some days before the scheduled session and will have prayed over it, marked places for prayer, and analyzed it pretty well. However, there are always items that will need further clarification and explanation.

I usually pray for a person for about two hours. The first item of business at hand is to pray and ask God's blessings upon the time we spend together. I pray that God will lead and guide us and bring to our minds anything that might need prayer that was not mentioned on the questionnaire.

Next I make a declaration to all evil spirits, commanding them not to manifest. The prayer will go something like this: "And now, in the mighty name of Jesus, I bind, muzzle and gag every evil spirit present in the heart and life of (name). I say you are forbidden to manifest or cause discomfort, and you will leave when I command you to do so! Holy Spirit, please come and accompany us as we pray together and guide all our thoughts, conversation and prayer, in Jesus' name."

The object of the next half hour is to place the person at ease. I usually have not seen the individual before, so I am a complete stranger. I try to act as much like a caring grandmother as I can, always trying to get to the bottom of things. Usually the main objective here is to locate the entry point(s), ascertain if someone needs to be forgiven and forge a "plan of attack" in my mind.

where do we start?

What we pray for first varies from case to case. As a rule, I start with the oldest problems from childhood, if there are any. Generally these have to do with inherited problems of rejection; problems that still hurt concerning family members, schoolmates, injustices and so forth. Then we cover the rest of the categories one at a time.

Occasionally you will run into persons whose special delight in life is going from counselor to counselor, talking about themselves and their problems. If their conversations are lengthy and they give you more detail than you need, politely tell them that you have enough information in the questionnaire and are looking for specific details concerning specific items. Sometimes, I'm convinced, the evil one wants to derail our thoughts or weary our minds so we don't stay sharp. It is important to keep control of the conversation and stay in charge of things.

I personally do not charge for my time. I feel that since I receive a salary, the ministry pays for my time. My board of directors has approved my praying deliverance over people as part of my job description. I also feel that the Scripture's injunction "Freely you have received, freely give" (Matt. 10:8) includes deliverance and praying for the sick, so I personally feel it is unacceptable to charge anyone. I have accepted spontaneous donations to the ministry, but I have not invited them, nor do I keep anything myself. Sometimes people like to give out of gratitude, and it would be wrong not to accept a gift for the ministry. It is sort of a "thanks offering" on their part.

Since I am giving them my time, I expect them to respect it and allow me to "call the shots." If anything gets too lengthy, I simply say something like, "My time is really limited, and in order to cover all the bases we will need to hurry along, so please let me ask a few more questions." Always be very kind in the way you say this, because some poor souls are already very rejected and a harsh reprimand is the last thing they need.

healing the memories

The last half hour is spent praying for healing of the memories and blessing the person. Everything I have marked in pink or every demon noted in a margin is prayed over, this time with the very opposite of the problem or stronghold. For example, if there was rage, I pray for quiet control in the person's mind and tongue. If there was hatred, I pray for love and so on.

Lastly, I pray a benediction over the person. I ask God to bless and keep them, bless their going out and their coming in, bless every aspect of their day-to-day life, and that the person would please the Lord in all they do, say and think.

I often get a rather strange comment as people are leaving. They frequently say something like, "I feel so light!" I have never actually gotten out a scale and weighed a demon, but apparently after a demon leaves an individual, there is a weight removed from the soul that makes the person feel lighter all over. And they like the new feeling.

I ask the person to write to me in about a month to let me know how things are progressing. I keep portions of these letters because they are so sweet—many of them give profuse thanks to the Lord for drastic changes in their lives that they never dreamed possible. Freedom sure beats bondage! Chapter 15 contains some of these anonymous testimonies.

In all honesty, this is something I would rather not do. While I dislike the process and listening to all the yucky things the devil does to people, I also must confess that I like to see what God can do to reverse all of that and bring freedom. Besides, the last time I looked in the Bible, I was still told to "cast out demons" (Matt 10:8; Mark 16:17). The best thing to say is, "Yes, Lord, I'll keep on doing it as long as I am able."

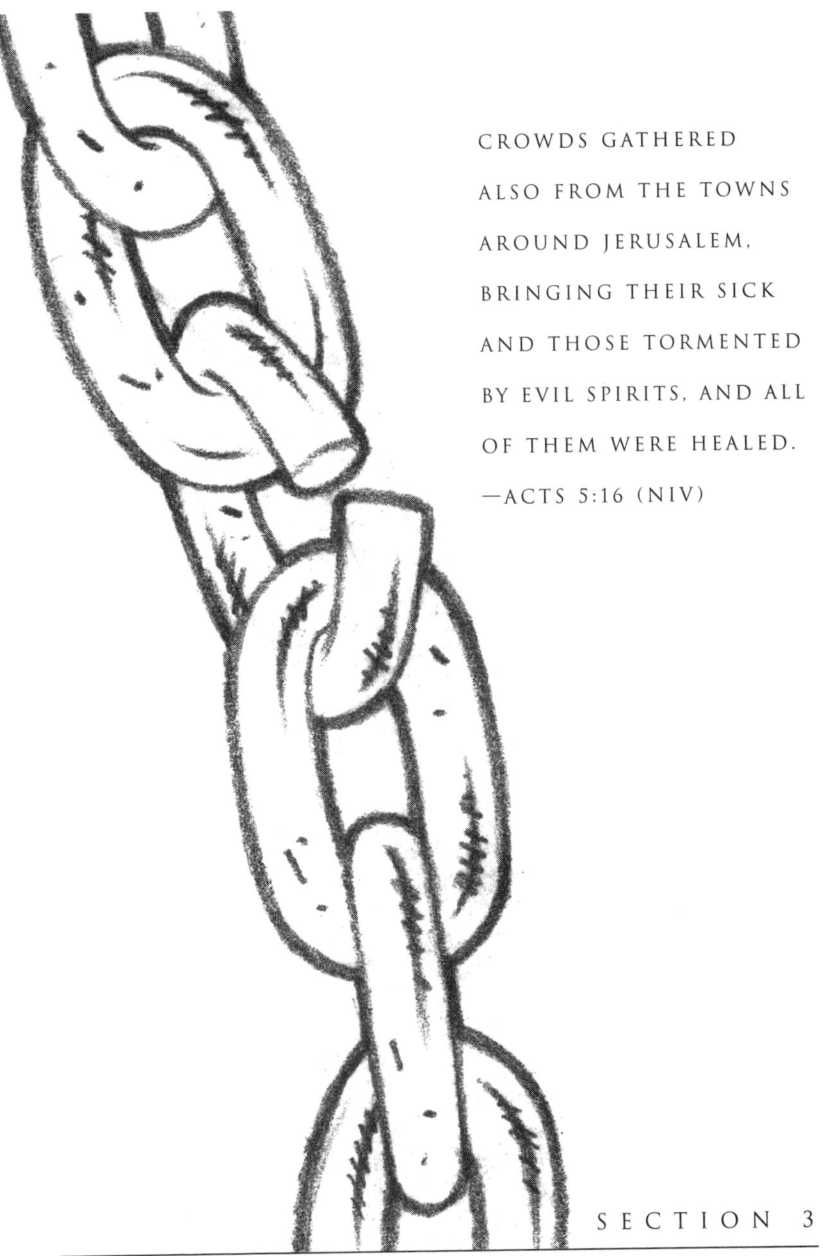

CROWDS GATHERED
ALSO FROM THE TOWNS
AROUND JERUSALEM,
BRINGING THEIR SICK
AND THOSE TORMENTED
BY EVIL SPIRITS, AND ALL
OF THEM WERE HEALED.
—ACTS 5:16 (NIV)

SECTION 3

the questionnaire as an effective tool

CHAPTER 9

collecting needed information

questionnaire, form letter and legal waiver

I am once again deeply indebted to Mrs. Phyl Gibson for allowing me to use the questionnaire prepared by her and her late husband, Noel. They have given permission to anyone who wishes to copy the content of the questionnaire to use in counseling sessions, so feel free to do so. Of course, a proper credit line must be included on each copy of the questionnaire, stating that it was taken from the book *Evicting Demonic Intruders* (Renew Books). It is illegal to reproduce it in any form to be sold.

This questionnaire has been a magnificent tool for me over the years. The purpose is to ask enough of the right questions to provide adequate information in locating problems and their sources. There are two other advantages. First, in order to get to the bottom of certain problems, detailed and embarrassing questions often need to be asked. If the answers are written out ahead of time, the information is already there and time has been saved. By going over some of the things the second time in the brief interview prior to the prayer, further details often surface that can prove very helpful.

The second advantage to using the questionnaire is that there may be several pages of questions that simply do not pertain to the session at hand, and all of that time can be saved. By having everything in writing, pieces fall into place very nicely. Over the years, I have noticed that most problems seem to fall in rather predictable patterns. The devil doesn't seem to invent much new. Once you've seen about 20 of these questionnaires, you've pretty much seen them all.

Remember, the question we ask ourselves over and over again as we examine the information is, Why are things the way they are? The next question to ask is, When did the problem begin? We are looking for entry points. I accompany the questionnaire with two items:

- a form letter from myself in which I inform them of my requirements and expectations;
- a legal waiver.

I ask them to sign the bottom of each document. Appendix 2 contains a sample that is available for use.

the session letter and legal waiver

The session letter must identify a number of critical points for the person who is requesting prayer and deliverance from demonic bondage.

1. This is only a prayer ministry and the person praying is not a psychological or medical professional.
2. There is no charge for the time.
3. The process may last two or more hours.
4. A signature must be given conveying consent that what the session entails is a voluntary request for prayer and a promise not to sue the parties involved who are praying for the deliverance.
5. Full disclosure and honesty is required.
6. Be prepared to forgive past or current individuals who may have hurt you. Unwillingness to do this may lead to a postponement of the session.
7. Before any appointment is set, you must promise to break with willful sin and bad habits, and you must truly desire deliverance from demonic oppression.
8. It is suggested that you fast before the day of the appointment; or if friends have been asked to attend, they fast and pray for those involved in the session.
9. Before any appointment begins, know that you may be asked to read the following supplication aloud (it may be read).

I confess Jesus Christ to be my personal Savior.
I renounce any oppression from the evil one in my life because of iniquity, transgression, and sin of my parents, ancestors or myself and humbly ask God for release and cleansing through the blood of Jesus Christ.

I repent from every sinful attitude, action or habit of mine which does not glorify Jesus Christ and ask forgiveness, release, cleansing and wholeness.

I renounce the devil and all demonic influences, bondages, dominations and infirmities in my life.

I ask You, Lord, for the release and freedom promised by Jesus Christ so that He may be Lord of my total personality and be glorified in all I say and do.
In His name I pray, amen.

10. As part of the completion to the form, identify to whom the document goes to at least 10 days before the scheduled appointment. All cancellations must be at least 24 hours in advance of the session.

Once the person has read the letter thoroughly the individual should sign, date, and note their name, address and phone on the form.

The second document I ask them to sign is a legal waiver. My lawyer drew up this document, and it may or may not be useful to you. I am requesting that if you use this document, please check it over with a lawyer from your state (or nation) to see if any corrections or additions need to be made. Please do not use it unless you have it reviewed. It may be submitted to your lawyer as a sample for guidance, if it is useful to him or her.

A sample copy of the legal waiver will also be found in Appendix 2 for your use, if you so desire.

I keep the two documents described above for my file. I do not keep the completed questionnaire or any notes that I have made before or during the session. After the prayer time is over and before the person leaves, I tear up the questionnaire and my notes in very small shreds in the presence of the person for whom

I prayed. This way, the person has the assurance that I am not filing any confidential information or sharing any of it with others.

the questionnaire

Now, let's move on to the questionnaire. I will give you a clean copy of the questionnaire in appendix 3 of this book so that you may reproduce it for your personal prayer sessions.

Occasionally there will be several possible afflicting spirits named. You should look for the words in the person's explanation that most closely fit the suggested names. This does not imply that if there are five possible afflicting spirits listed, the person is in bondage to all five of those spirits. The suggested names are for your guidance and help as you are starting out. There may be other names besides those listed, of course. Call out the name of the spirit that is afflicting the person by the symptom it produces and command it to leave in the name of Jesus. For example:

Spirit of fear of rejection,
in Jesus' name, I bind you, I break your power,
and I command you to loose this sister and let her go now.

The appendix copy of the questionnaire will have enough space for the person to write in their answers. My suggestion is that it be enlarged in order to have ample space for writing in the responses or retyped to be more attractive and user-friendly.

prayer ministry questionnaire

This form opens up in a standard format and asks for the person's name, age, marital status and profession. The person is then asked several questions.

In this whole section we are trying to really gain an understanding of the depth of the person's Christian conversion and walk with the Lord. If the person is not a believer in Christ, the first order of business before deliverance is to lead that one to Jesus as Savior.

The person is asked to answer the following questions briefly:

1. What is your church background?
2. Explain briefly your conversion experience. If you came to Christ as a teenager or older, was your life really changed?
3. Were you baptized as a child? Were you baptized as an adult?
4. In one word, who is Jesus Christ to you?
5. What does the blood of Calvary mean to you?
6. Is repentance part of your Christian life?
7. What is your prayer life like?
8. Do you have assurance of salvation?
9. Do you have a problem with doubt and unbelief in everyday Christian living?
10. Are you satisfied with your Christian walk? If not, how would you like to see it improve?

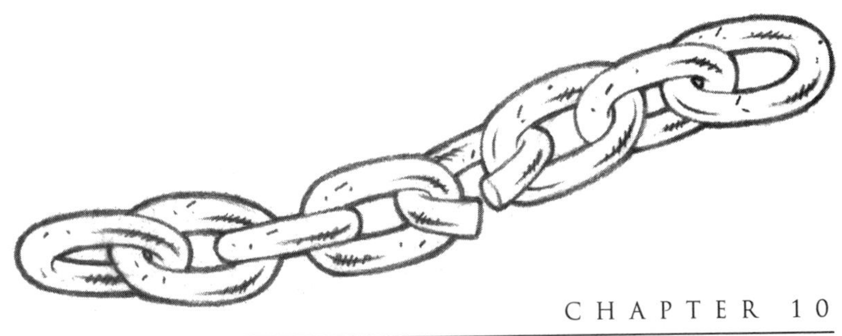

CHAPTER 10

rejection issues

In **Category A** of the questionnaire the subject is on rejection issues. It would be helpful for you to refer to the illustration of the rejection tree in chapter 5 and maybe even keep a photocopy handy.

In this chapter and in the remaining ones to follow, I have attempted to provide clarification and teaching on certain questions used in the inquiry process. All the questions listed in this chapter and through chapter 14 are in bold type. Occasionally, a question will be followed by my personal suggestions which are identified in plain text. Finally, it is important to note: *The following sample questions are abbreviated and condensed from the longer, functional version of the questionnaire found in Appendix 3.*

1. Was your relationship with your parents good, bad or indifferent?

2a. Were you a planned child?

Children who were not wanted or planned can suffer rejection from the womb, especially if the news of the pregnancy was met with remorse and spoken words of something like "I don't want this child."

2b. Were You the "right" sex?

It is possible for a child to act like a person of the sex desired if the parents were very disappointed with the gender of the child. For example, a girl may choose a very masculine vocation in a subconscious attempt to please the parents. If this seems to be a problem, I tell the person that God does not make mistakes and that He made the person exactly the way He wanted. This item needs prayer only if the person senses rejection because of his or her gender, and especially if the parents reminded the child throughout growing up that they wanted a child of the opposite sex. In this case, forgiveness needs to be extended to the parents for their insensitivity and a spirit of rejection needs to be cast out. Many times the individual is very well adjusted to their gender and does not feel a sense of rejection from the parents. In this case, the above information is only an explanation of why certain personality traits have taken place. Don't make a big deal out of a nonexistent problem!

2c. Were you conceived out of wedlock?

Persons conceived out of wedlock or as the result of rape can suffer from the effects of demons that take advantage of the situation. Frequently, those conceived in lust will struggle with lust during their lifetime. Those conceived during trauma can suffer from spirits of lust, violence, anger and an assortment of fears.

2d. Were you adopted?

Adopted children frequently become very rebellious and difficult to handle. I have usually been led to cast out a spirit of abandonment residing in adopted kids. They need to pray to forgive their birth parents for giving them away. I then pray that God will cause them to be grateful for their adoptive parents and bond with them as though they were the natural parents. Check out the fruit of the rejection tree and pray concerning each symptom noted. Pray against hereditary rejection since you probably won't know about the past; and usually fear of rejection, perceived rejection and their own root of rejection need to be cast out.

2e. If adopted, do you know anything about your natural parents?

Frequently there are very good reasons why a child is given up for adoption. I once prayed with a man who found out that his mother had a terminal illness and she wanted her son to have a much better chance at life than she could give. Reasons are not always selfish, and sometimes the best interests of the child are upheld. Given today's shocking abortion rates, any child carried to term usually has some careful thought behind the decision. Frequently, of course, it is a case of an unwanted child with strong rejection and bonding issues with which to deal.

2f. Do you know if your mother suffered any trauma during her pregnancy with you?

Spirits of trauma, violence and even death can enter during pregnancy, especially if the mother was a battered wife. Somehow the child can feel to blame for the problems. Rejection results.

2g. Do you know if you suffered a difficult or complicated birth?

Sometimes spirits of trauma, violence, panic and the like take advantage of a situation where there is a struggle for life, when instruments are used for delivery, or the umbilical cord is around the neck.

2h. Were you "bonded at birth"?

2i. Were you a breast-fed baby?

2j. Do you have brothers and sisters? Where do you fall in the sibling line? How was your relationship with them growing up? What is it like now? Are there any special problems?
We are attempting to discover if there were factors in the family home that might be a root of rejection—such as one child favored over another.

3. Are your parents living? Are they Christians? Living together? Divorced?
If a parent, sibling or whoever might be the felt cause of some rejection issue has died, the person can still pray and tell the Lord that he or she is willing to forgive, even though the individual is gone.

How old were you when they divorced? Is your father or mother remarried? If remarried, how is your relationship with your stepfather or stepmother? Is your stepfather or stepmother a Christian? Are there stepbrothers or stepsisters? How was your relationship with them while growing up? How is your relationship now?
Someone may need to be forgiven for hurtful behavior and rejection.

Are you a critical person?
Look for a generational critical spirit as well.

5. Do you feel emotionally immature?
If yes, pray against a spirit of emotional immaturity.

6. Tell us about your self-image. Do you have a low self-image, feelings of insecurity, self-condemnation, hatred of yourself, feelings of worthlessness, feelings of being a failure, a sense of inferiority, questions of identity or desires to punish yourself?
Here you may need to pray against spirits of self-condemnation, hopelessness, despair, self-punishment, etc.

7. Was your father passive or strong and manipulative? Briefly describe your relationship with your father.
You may need to pray against a spirit of manipulation and control.

8. Was your mother passive or strong and manipulative? Briefly describe your relationship with your mother.
Manipulation and control again.

9. Was yours a happy home during childhood?

10. How would you describe your family's financial situation when you were a child? Poor? Slight financial struggles? Moderate income? Affluent?
Spirits of poverty, shame, greed, materialism.

11. Has lying or stealing been a problem to you? Is it now?
Spirits of lying, deceit, kleptomania, stealing.

12. Were you lonely as a teenager?
Spirits of loneliness, grief, abandonment.

13. As a child or teenager or later in life, did you ever suffer an injustice?

Children can carry scars for life because of an injustice. It may be a seemingly insignificant insult or theft or being cheated out of something. However, spirits may have entered such as anger, rejection, shame, grief, bitterness, resentment, unforgiveness, etc. The individuals must be forgiven first, as usual.

14. Do you have trouble giving or receiving love?

Spirits of emotional coldness. Break bondages over emotions.

15. Do you find it easy to communicate with persons close to you?

16. Are you a perfectionist? Were (are) your parents perfectionists?

Spirits of hereditary perfectionism, rejection, stress.

17. Do you come from a proud family?

A generational spirit of pride.

18. Do you personally have a problem with pride?

Spirits of pride, arrogance, self-aggrandizement.

19. Do you have or have you had problems with impatience, irritability, temper, racial prejudice, moodiness, rebellion, violence, stubbornness, anger and temptation to murder?

This is a grouping of symptoms from the rejection tree with others added. It helps to see if self-rejection and aggressive rejection are problems. Pray about each one, then add self-rejection or aggression, if necessary.

20. Have you been given to swearing, blasphemies, obscenities? Do you swear, blaspheme or use obscenities now?
These are from the rebellious/aggressive branches of the tree.

21. Do you have unforgiveness toward anyone? Resentment? Bitterness? Hatred?
Here, persons need to be forgiven. Sometimes soul-ties need to be broken and these spirits evicted. Be sure to pray for the healing of wounded memories at the end.

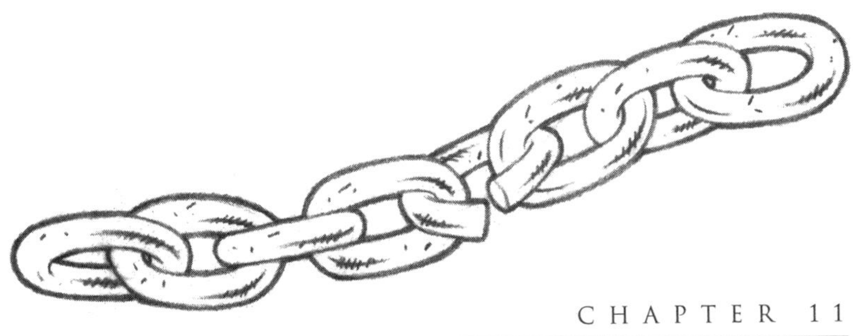

CHAPTER 11

mental and emotional problems

Category B deals with mental and emotional problems.

1. Are you easily frustrated? Do you show it or bury it?

2. Are you an anxious person, a worrier or someone who gets depressed?
Spirits of anxiety, worry or depression.

3. Did either of your parents suffer from depression?
Spirits of generational depression or nervous breakdown.

4. Has any parent, brother, sister, or grandparent suffered from acute nervousness or a mental problem?
Some mental problems may be tied in with evil spirits. Others may not, but may be caused by some physical problems such as

chemical imbalances, deformities, injuries and the like. If you feel like the problem is demon related, some spirits to look for might be schizophrenia, manic depression, a spirit of mental illness, confusion, etc.

Always pray for physical healing along with spiritual healing, when needed. Remember, Jesus said to preach the gospel, heal the sick and cast out demons all in the same breath! (See Matt. 10:8.)

5. Have you personally ever had psychiatric counseling? Hospitalization? Shock treatment? Psychoanalysis? Other?
At times, people in mental hospitals are treated badly and opportunity for spirits of trauma, anger, victimization, deception, and the like are opened.

6. Have you ever been hypnotized? If so, when and why?
Hypnosis can be an opening for evil spirits to take advantage of a person at a time when he or she is not in control of the mind. Often a mental condition will worsen after hypnosis. If it does, I pray this way: "Now I address every evil spirit that took advantage of (John's) hypnotic state and entered at that time. I bind you all, I break your power, and I command you to loose (John) and let him go, now." There may also be spirits of mind control and confusion.

7. Have you had advanced education?
People can educate themselves into unbelief. Our educational system of secular humanism has a way of doing this to some not strong in the faith. Problems can be skepticism, unbelief, argumentative spirit, intellectual pride, arrogance.

8. Have you, your parents or your grandparents been in any

of the following cults: Christian Science, Rosicrucian, Jehovah's Witnesses, Mormonism, Unification Church (Moonies), Unity, Spiritist churches, Children of Love, Scientology, Christadelphians, Bahai, religious communes, Theosophy, Native American religions, gurus or Eastern religions such as Hinduism, Buddhism (Zen, Tibetan), Islam, etc.? Other?

These cults and faiths can let in spirits of false religion. Name the spirit by the name of the cult.

9. To your knowledge, has any close family member been a Freemason, Oddfellow, Rainbow Girl, Mormon, Eastern Star, Shriner, Daughter of the Nile, Job's Daughter, Elk or De Molay? Do you suffer from apathy, hardness of emotion, confusion, financial disaster, skepticism, doubt, unbelief, comprehension difficulty, infirmities, frequent sickness, allergies and mockery?

The above can be symptoms of Freemason curses. Be sure to review chapter 10 of *Evicting Demonic Intruders* if there is Freemasonry in the person's background. When evicting this spirit, name it the "spirit of Freemasonry and the Luciferan doctrine." Other spirits can be witchcraft, antichrist, confusion, poltergeist, false religion and above-mentioned symptoms. After dealing with the above-mentioned spirits that apply, be sure to give a copy of the prayer for ex-Freemasons and their descendants to the individual to pray over at home. The prayer is located in appendix 5 of this book.

Is there any Masonic regalia or memorabilia in your possession?

All regalia and memorabilia must be destroyed. If a ring is solid gold and can be melted down, it can be made into something else. Remember, the children of Israel made all of the gold items for the tabernacle in the wilderness for the worship of Jehovah God from the gold and jewelry they had taken from the Egyptians. This must have included items fashioned after the gods of the Egyptians. When the symbolism is destroyed, the gold can be melted down and purified. It then simply reverts to the beautiful precious metal that God created. I believe it inadvisable to keep a Masonic Bible, because of their view of the Scriptures (pick a religion, any religion; pick a sacred writing, any will do; they all lead to the same place). Besides, it may have been used in some pagan ceremony at the Lodge or elsewhere.

10. Do you feel mentally confused? Have mental blocks?
Spirit of confusion.

11. Do you daydream? Have mental fantasies?
Spirits of mental fantasy or escapism.

12. Do you suffer from frequent bad dreams? Sleeplessness?
Spirits of death, violence, fear or lust (depending upon the theme of the dreams).

13. Have you ever been tempted to commit suicide? Have you tried? If yes, how, when and why?

14. Have you ever wished to die? Spoken it aloud?
Questions 13 and 14 have to do with a spirit of death and suicide. If the person has wished to die and spoken it aloud, it is a "death wish" curse and the curse must be broken first. The person prays and asks forgiveness for wishing he or she were dead and speaking it aloud. It is done something like this: "In the name of Jesus, I break the power of that death wish, and,

through the blood of Jesus, I cancel every curse of death over (name). This one will no longer wish to die but will wish to live, in Jesus' name."

15. Have you had a strong and prolonged fear of any of the following: failure, inability to cope, inadequacy, authority figures, the dark, death, rape, violence, being alone, Satan and evil spirits, the future, women, crowds, heights, men, insanity, public speaking, accidents, the opinions of people, old age, death or injury of a loved one, enclosed places, terminal illness, divorce or marriage breakup, insects, spiders, dogs, snakes, animals, water, pain, loud noises, flying in an airplane, open spaces and/or grocery stores?

Since becoming a Christian, do any of the above fears still grip you?

I then pray over every fear the person lists as being present *after* becoming a Christian—by name, such as "You spirit of fear of spiders, in Jesus' name, I bind you, I break your power, and I command you to loose (name) and let (him, her) go now."

After praying over each fear, I address the general spirit of fear that has manifested itself in the fears listed. The prayer is the same, except I address, "You spirit of fear . . ."

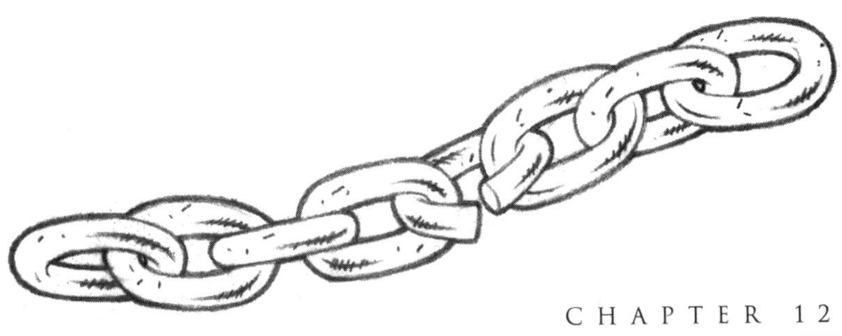

CHAPTER 12

witchcraft and the occult

Category C deals with witchcraft and the occult.

1. Have you ever made a pact with the devil? Was it a blood pact? Are you willing to renounce it?

What does a "pact with the devil" sound like? It is simply a deal that a person makes with the devil that exchanges his or her soul for a favor, frequently money, power or love. It would sound something like this: "I will forever burn in hell if you will give me the love of Tom." Sometimes it is accompanied by extracting drops of blood from the body. When there have been curses spoken or vows taken at witches' coven meetings, or at satanic worship services, these are frequently accompanied with the drinking of potions of the blood of some sacrifice and other material such as urine or some other substance. The vows or pacts made in this manner, particularly when accompanied by the use of blood, are very strong. However, the blood of Jesus is much more powerful.

When I am praying with a person who has made a pact with the devil, the first order of business is to renounce the pact. By renouncing, we mean to "take back the words spoken." For example, in the above case, a woman named Susie would say, "I renounce the words 'I will forever burn in hell if you will give me the love of Tom.'" Then I would declare, "And now, through the blood of Jesus, which is more powerful than the blood used in this pact, I declare that pact null and void—it has no more power over Susie. I say that curse is broken over her and has no more effect in her life, in the name of Jesus. In Jesus' name, I pray total cleansing over her body and complete purification from the contamination of the potion she drank."

2. To your knowledge, has any curse been placed on you or your family?

Here, the person would pray to forgive the one placing the curse and ask God's mercy on the one who did it. I would break the curse, similar to the way it was done above.

3. To your knowledge, have your parents or any relative as far back as you know been involved in occultism or witchcraft?

If there has been witchcraft in the family background, the person needs to forgive the one who let the opening into the family line. We then cast out a spirit of generational witchcraft.

4. Have you ever had involvement with any of the following: fortune-tellers, tarot cards, Ouija boards, séances, mediums, palmistry, astrology, color therapy, levitation, astral travel, horoscope, lucky charms, black magic, demon worship, asked for a spirit guide, clairvoyance, crystals, done automatic

handwriting, New Age movement, been to a curandero or native healer? Have you been involved in any other witchcraft, demonic or satanic things?

The above-listed items can be openings for spirits of witchcraft, fear and death. Children are frequently trapped into spirits of death and fear by playing "ghost stories" and calling up the dead in what they think is just a make-believe séance. But when the dead are called up, evil spirits can take advantage of the situation and spirits of death and fear can contaminate some of the children for life. When something in the room moves, fear can grip a child and it can even become panic. In some cases, the child becomes fascinated with the experience and delves further into witchcraft. So, look for some of the above-mentioned items as entry points, even if the person claimed to be doing the activity in jest or "didn't mean anything by it."

Ouija boards are a common opening for an entrance of a spirit of fear and witchcraft. I was told in one of my seminars that in 1997 there were 7 million Ouija boards sold in the U.S. alone. When I am Christmas shopping for my grandchildren, if I encounter a Ouija board in a store, I pick up a Monopoly or Sorry game and place it in front of the Ouija board to get it out of sight. They are very demonic!

If the person has been involved in any of the above, he or she prays and asks forgiveness for their involvement in (name of involvement), and we cast out a spirit of witchcraft and often death, fear and a few others that may come to mind.

5. Have you ever read books on occultism or witchcraft?

If the reason was to learn to throw curses on someone or to worship Satan, or the like, repentance must be performed. Any item, such as a satanic bible, must be destroyed, since it has been used in idolatrous worship. Some Christians think they should learn about the enemy in order to serve the Lord better and they attempt to read certain occultic books. It is unwise to delve into these, since the material can contaminate the mind. If, for some special reason, material of this sort needs to be read, pray protection over your mind before doing it and pray cleansing over the mind after. When the person read such books for knowledge or pleasure before becoming a Christian, I pray cleansing over the mind. I suggest these materials be burned.

Science fiction can contain witchcraft and occult themes and detailed descriptions and information not edifying to a Christian. I suggest that these be avoided.

6. Have you played demonic games such as Dungeons & Dragons? Watched demonic films? Do you now?

Destroy all materials. Spirits of death, suicide and fear often accompany the use of such things.

7. Have you been involved in transcendental meditation? Do you have a mantra? If so, what is it?

To give you an example of a mantra, I was once praying for a young man who was struggling with a strong spirit of lust. In his junior college he had taken a course in transcendental meditation and been given a mantra. I asked what it was, and he said it was just a couple of syllables he was to repeat over and over as he meditated. The Lord led me to ask him to copy it down, and I took it to a friend of mine from India and asked her if she knew the meaning of the word. She looked horrified and said it was the name of a filthy sexual goddess of Hinduism. As he was "meditating," he was calling up this lustful demon. No wonder he was struggling with lust! At his invitation, she had established a tormenting foothold in his life. I asked him to pray, asking God's forgiveness for studying transcendental meditation, and once he had renounced the mantra, we dispatched the spirit of lust.

8. Have you been involved in Eastern religions? Followed a guru?

Once again, renounce the involvement, being as specific as possible, and pledge allegiance to God the Father, Jesus Christ His Son, our Savior, and the Holy Spirit as our Comforter.

9. Have you ever visited heathen temples? Made offerings? What were they? Did you take part in any ceremony?

If these involvements were part of worship, once again follow the instructions in question 8. If any negative symptoms such as fears, nightmares or the like started after visiting a temple, pray cleansing. Sometimes students are required to visit a temple in conjunction with the study of comparative religions classes. I certainly recommend praying protection over yourself before entering, and cleansing over yourself after leaving. Never take part in any ceremonies or offerings or spin prayer wheels or the like. And while there, pray God's mercy on those people who are worshiping demons or idols, that they would find the truth in Christ.

10. Have you ever done any form of yoga? Meditation? Exercises?

Renounce these religious exercises, meditations and worship times. Cast out religious spirits of yoga.

11. Have you ever learned or used any form of mind communication or mind control?

Repent and cast out spirits of mind control, ESP, mind dynamics, and confusion.

12. Were your parents or grandparents superstitious? Were or are you?
This can be an opening for generational spirits of witchcraft.

13. Have you ever worn lucky charms, fetishes, amulets or signs of the zodiac? Do you have any in your possession?
Be sure to have the person go through their jewelry boxes and clean out all such objects. They should be burned or otherwise totally destroyed. Many are cursed objects and can bring demons with them. Repentance, renunciation and cleansing are in order. Cast out spirits of witchcraft.

14. Do you have in your home any symbols of idols or spirit worship, such as Buddhas, totem poles, painted face masks, idol carvings, fetishes, pagan symbols, native art (if so, what kind?), tikis or Kachina dolls? Where are they from and how did you get them?
All such items need curses broken and must be destroyed, preferably smashed and burned. A problem can arise when the idols belong to a relative living in the same home. You have the right to destroy only what is yours. You can point out to the owner that you are a Christian and will not give allegiance to idols. If the person is a guest in your home, you may request that they be kept in the other person's quarters. If you are the guest and the idols belong to your parents, for example, you should pray protection over yourself and command demons to leave you alone. You should pray cleansing over your room, anoint the doors, windows, your bed, etc. with oil and command evil spirits to depart. Ask the Lord to spiritually "seal it off," fill it with the presence of the Holy Spirit and not allow evil spirits to enter.

15. Do you have any witches, such as "good-luck kitchen witches," in your home?

No witches are good witches. They represent evil and have no place in the home of a believer in Christ.

16. Are you "turned on" by any of the following music: rock and roll, punk rock, New Age, rap, heavy metal?

It is very wise to destroy that which has lyrics encouraging sin, such as perverse or illicit sexual behavior, violence, suicide and bad language.

17. Have you ever learned any of the martial arts? Do you practice it now?

Martial arts are linked with Buddhism. They are frequently an opening for spirits of anger, violence, revenge and murder. The practice should be abandoned.

18. Have you ever had premonitions? Déjà vu? Psychic sight?

Déjà vu that has occurred possibly once or twice a few years ago is not a concern to me. However, premonitions, psychic sight and déjà vu that pops up more often needs prayer. Look for spirits of deception, psychic sight, déjà vu, sorcery and witchcraft.

19. Have you ever been involved in firewalking, voodoo, any other form of religious pagan ceremony?

These need repentance, renunciation and curses broken.

20. Do you have any tattoos?

I am sure you have seen very demonic-looking tattoos on the bodies of men and women of all ages. When a person becomes a

Christian, most would agree that demonic and satanic symbolism on that person's body is not in order. It is recommended that laser surgery remove such tattoos. They can create a bondage to the symbolism they represent and can stand in the way of total freedom in Christ. It is interesting that Leviticus 19:28 in the *New King James Version* says, "You shall not make any cuttings in your flesh for the dead, nor tattoo any marks on you. I am the Lord." This verse is in the midst of a passage teaching against sorcery, divination, soothsaying, mediums and familiar spirits. Hmm . . .

There just might be some connection.

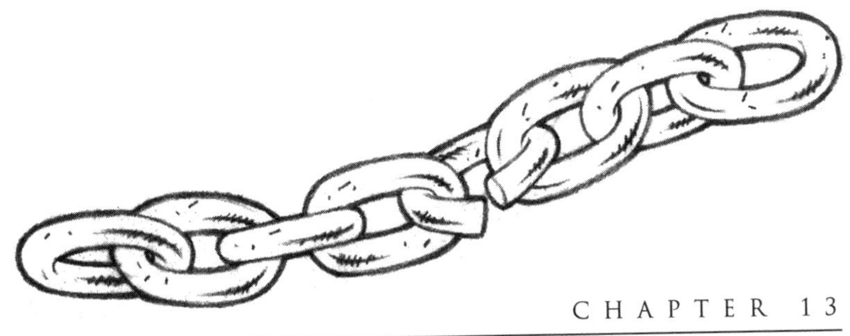

CHAPTER 13

lust and sexual bondages

Category D deals with spirits of lust and sexual bondages.

1. Do you have lustful thoughts? Frequency?

2. To your knowledge, was there evidence of lust in your parents, grandparents or further back?

Here we are attempting to discover if there is also a generational spirit of lust lurking about. These are very common. I have found it helpful to cut off a generational spirit of lust, then complete this whole section of Category D, dealing up front with each personal sexual bondage. Lastly I go for the "strongman" in this category with: "And now you spirit of lust, in Jesus' name, I bind you, I break your power, and I command you to loose this brother and let him go NOW, in the name of Jesus Christ of Nazareth–be gone!"

3. Do you frequently masturbate? Do you know why? Do you feel it is a compulsive problem?

Occasional masturbation is frequently a part of growing up. If it becomes a controlling habit, there is probably a demonic bondage attached. Compulsive masturbation can be an addiction that interferes with marriage and produces guilt and shame. I have prayed for men who have been in the habit of masturbating several times a day. If this is a problem, we cast out a spirit of masturbation and fantasy lust. Look for a spirit of addiction, as well, in severe cases and cast out guilt and shame.

4. Were you ever sexually molested by someone outside your family as a child or teenager? By whom? More than once? Were you actually raped?

5. Have you ever been a victim of incest by a family member?

6. Men: Have you ever molested or raped anyone? Names. Committed incest? Women: Have you ever been raped? Names.

We frequently discover that much sexual bondage is rooted "way back when" at the time of a molestation of some sort. Questions 4, 5 and 6 all deal with collecting information on these unfortunate events. The person needs to forgive the guilty one, or forgive himself or herself for victimizing another. Of course, necessary amends are in order for the victimizer where appropriate. Molesters were often molested themselves, so look for generational spirits of molestation, lust, incest, etc.

As was explained previously, sometimes the victim needs to forgive God for what is believed to be abandonment at the time of victimization.

We need to look for spirits of lust, defilement, hatred, incest, anger, guilt, shame, unforgiveness, bitterness, a man-hating spirit and the like.

7. Have you ever committed fornication (single persons)? How many partners? First names and when. With prostitutes? How many? When? Have you ever committed adultery (at least one partner married)? First name(s) and when. Are you currently involved in an illicit sexual relationship? Are you willing to break it off?

8. Have you ever had homosexual or lesbian desires? Do you now? Experience?

Sexual sins and victimizations are different from other sins (see 1 Cor. 6:12-20). The physical body of the person is "sinned against." This needs to be cleaned up in order for a proper marriage relationship to be enjoyed. I ask for the names of those involved with incidents of fornication, prostitution, adultery, homosexual or lesbian liaisons, as well as incestuous and victimization occurrences. I do not enjoy collecting this information. The purpose is to break unholy soul-ties with each of those individuals. I command the soul-tie to be broken in a prayer something like this:

And now, in the mighty name of Jesus,
I break all ungodly ties of body, soul and spirit
between you and (insert name).
I ask God to draw back to you every part
that was placed in bondage to (insert name).
I now speak to every evil spirit that took
advantage of this ungodly soul-tie
and I command you to leave now in Jesus' name.
I forbid you to afflict any other member of this person's family.

In the case of homosexuality, I often get the phrase, "But I was born this way." My answer is usually, "You probably were. My question to you is, 'Do you want to stay that way or be free to be normal?'" I would go after a generational spirit of homosexuality, then his own spirit of homosexuality, or in the case of a woman the corresponding spirit of lesbianism. Soul-ties need to be broken, of course.

Defiled skin, sexual organs, eyes, ears, etc.—all need cleansing prayers when sexual problems are cleaned up in the spirit. I also pray a prayer of dedication of these body parts to the Lord, for proper and normal use. It is also good to pray for proper sexual male and female roles to be assumed in each, that men would be fully masculine, as God intended, and women would be fully feminine in the same way.

9. Are you sexually frigid (married women only)?

Look for spirits of resentment, bitterness, frigidity, emotional coldness.

10. Have you ever sexually fantasized about an animal? Committed a sex act (bestiality) with an animal? Name all animals involved:

Cast out a spirit of *(the name of the animal)*. Also bestiality, guilt, shame.

11. Has pornography ever attracted you? How did you become involved? Have you seen porn movies? Videos? Live sex shows? Do you currently purchase or rent porn, or have such a channel on your home TV?

Pornography is highly addictive. Images seem to be seared in the mind and impossible to erase—they keep coming back. If this was a willful sin on the part of the person you are praying with, that person needs to pray something like: "Lord, forgive me for getting into pornography. I repent and ask you to cleanse me from its contamination and free me from this bondage."

If the person was "victimized" by finding porn in Dad's room, or by Uncle Harry's having left it available or the teenager next door showing the person his video or magazine, then the one asking for prayer needs to forgive the one who led him or her into the bondage, before praying a prayer similar to the one in the above paragraph.

Look for spirits of pornography, sexual fantasy and addiction. Pray for cleansing from images seared in the memory. Ask God to remove them, and press the "delete" button of the brain regarding these pictures.

Instruct the person to destroy all materials, such as books, magazines, photos, videos, etc. Also, cable TV channels must be canceled. Sometimes pictures are scrambled on these channels, but the voice is as clear as a bell. This is not helpful. Demand that the channel be removed from the box. If internet is a problem, it should be blocked, as it is for children.

12. Have you ever been involved in oral sex? With whom?

Oral sex with anyone outside of marriage is an opening for perverse sexual spirits to create bondages. These need to be expelled and those parts of the body involved need a prayer of cleansing. There is a difference of opinion, even on the part of prominent Christian counselors, as to whether occasional, mutually acceptable, oral stimulation within marriage is okay. Frankly, I have no opinion. I would say, however, that if a husband demands something that is repulsive or offensive to the wife, it is out of order and should be abandoned. The feelings of the wife are very important and must be respected. If oral sex within marriage were requested by the husband to replace normal sex, I would suspect that a perverse spirit has entered and it needs to be expelled. Sometimes good Christian marriage counseling is in order if things don't go smoothly after prayer. Bad habits, bad manners or poor communication skills can be corrected, if parties are willing to do so.

13. Have you been involved in anal sex? With whom?

Sodomy is condemned throughout Scripture. Forgiveness needs to be extended where necessary and cleansing prayed over the body. All spirits of homosexuality and sodomy as well as degradation and possible rejection need to be cast out. We see how God judged Sodom for its reputation, and the first chapter of Romans recaps God's feelings on the subject for us in the New Testament. The rules for Christians seem inescapable to me. This is a definite no-no as well as being the most commonly known method of transferring the HIV virus.

14. Women: Have you ever had an abortion? How many? Give dates and name(s) of father(s). Men: Have you ever fathered a child that was forcefully aborted? How many? Give dates and name(s) of mother(s).

The emotional damage caused by having an abortion can last for years, if not a whole lifetime. Self-forgiveness and forgiveness extended to the father need to take place before one can pray for cleansing and wholeness. Spirits to look for are murder, death, grief, unforgiveness, resentment, bitterness, a man-hating spirit, self-hatred and rejection.

I always pray for healing of the womb after a murder has taken place there. Sometimes, frigidity in marriage can be traced back to an abortion. Occasionally a woman needs to hear that the baby is with the Lord, that she will see it someday and that God has forgiven this sin.

Men who have insisted on the abortion of a child they have fathered are really accomplices to murder when it comes right down to it. They, too, need to repent and ask for forgiveness. Look for spirits of lust, abandonment, murder, emotional cruelty and rape (if it applies).

15. Have you been plagued with desires of having sex with a child (pedophilia)? Have you actually done so?

If a person has been plagued with this desire, by all means cast out a spirit of pedophilia. Some Christians struggle with spirits but have not given in to them. A person with this spirit probably picked it up through inheritance, pornography, or having been victimized as a child.

If a person has actually been a child abuser and the authorities do not know about it, it is your duty to report it, in most cases. This is a crime. Be sure the person you are praying for knows you need to do this. If other Christians are involved, they may choose not to press charges if convinced that the guilty one is healed and that the victim has been prayed for and healed emotionally and in every other respect. It is probably proper to go to the person's pastor first and have him or her deal with the authorities. This is a very delicate and difficult problem, but my advice is to obey the law and start with your pastor. The person should turn himself over to legal authorities, in my opinion, and make all amends possible.

I personally have never had to do this (thank God!), but I did have one man cancel an appointment with me. I wondered if this might not have been the problem, but was never told. This is one of the ways the devil keeps child abusers in business—they must either run or turn themselves over. I would love to see them healed! Often this can only occur after they are caught and incarcerated, but better late than never.

16. Have you ever had inner sexual stimulation and climax out of your control, especially at night? By this I mean, do you have dreams of a personage approaching and asking to have sex with you, or just doing it, and you "feel" a presence in bed with you, then wake up with a sexual climax? (This is something other than a normal nocturnal emission.)

This problem is caused by lustful spirits who approach a person in a dream and cause sexual stimulation after having asked permission. Once given permission, they can freely return. They especially enjoy working in the darkness, but are often bold enough to cause problems in the day as well. If the spirit is female in nature, its name is Succubus. If it acts like a male, its name is Incubus. Call it by its name when evicting it. I have dealt with these spirits that have been in family lines for generations.

Sometimes they enter through witchcraft ceremonies or satanic worship. Look also for spirits of lust, guilt and demonic mind control. They frequently give a jolt to the body when called by name. I suspect they are shocked that they are known by their rightful names.

17. Have you ever gone to a massage parlor and been sexually stimulated?

Look for spirits of pornography, sexual fantasy, lust, etc. Pray cleansing over every part of the body touched by the masseuse or masseur.

18. How would you describe your sexual relationship with your spouse?

I believe that sex is given to married couples for total enjoyment. If this is not the case, I try to locate spiritual causes for problems and pray about them. When there have been sexual sins, God's original plan has been corrupted and repair is needed.

Sometimes, even after prayer, counseling is needed to change stubborn patterns and manners. I find that women are often guilty of using sex as a weapon, by withholding it for their own purposes. I counsel that this is wrong and remind them that Scripture says they are to share their body with their husband.

I also find that some men are unkind, demanding and careless. When it comes to having the skills to be romantic, they are clueless. Our society has so conditioned men that they often demand sex from the time they are teenagers and are determined to get it at whatever cost. Romance for many is unknown because they don't have role models in their homes. A huge problem is that they confuse love with sex, and I often see the words used interchangeably. No wonder they are all mixed up! Both men and women often can't quite understand the love of God or Christ's love for humanity because their definition of the word "love" is blurred. (I get the impression that when some folks use the phrase "intimacy with Christ," they have some raging sexual experience in mind, because perhaps real love, romance and intimacy have different definitions in their minds. In my mind, this intimacy with Christ means being special people alone with Him, as were His inner circle of disciples.)

Cindy Jacobs once told me of a bizarre incident in which a spirit of Incubus approached a woman, telling her that he was Jesus wanting to have intimate relations with her. The woman was convinced that she was having "intimacy with Christ." But when she looked into the eyes of this thing, she realized she had been deceived and it was a lying demon. Fortunately, she sought help and it was expelled. This is another reason why I shy away from the phrase "intimacy with Christ" when it smacks of sexual overtones, especially with women involved.

The closest intimacy with Christ I see in Scripture is John leaning on Jesus' chest and Jesus calling him His beloved disciple. I believe we can and should gain this close fellowship with Him, but in my mind, it is not sexual. I realize that we are His bride, but we are not yet His wife, nor are we "all present and accounted for," since the task of world evangelization is not yet complete.

When these problems occur, after bondages have been prayed over in both partners, I would suggest giving it a little time. If there are still problems with settling into a pleasant sexual marriage experience, refer the couple to a good Christian marriage counselor.

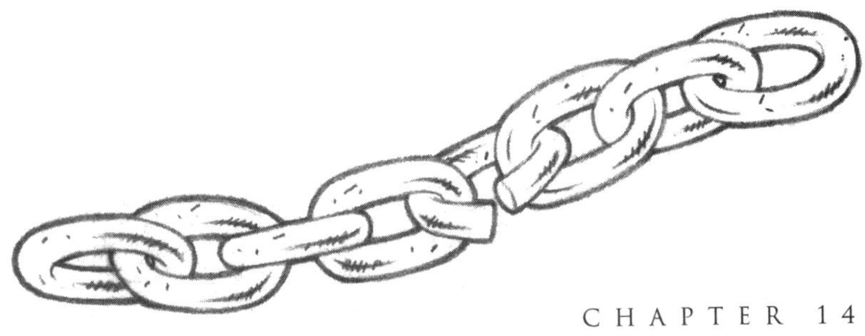

CHAPTER 14

addictions, background issues and miscellaneous

Category E deals with addictions.

1. Did any of your family, as far back as you know, have addictions of any kind?

2. Have you ever been addicted to any of the following: alcohol, smoking, food, gambling, compulsive exercise, being a spendthrift, watching TV, coffee, drugs (prescribed or hallucinatory)? Are any of the above a current problem?

The same spirit of addiction can manifest in different ways. There is frequently a generational spirit of addiction that needs to be dealt with. I like to tell the spirit of addiction that its assignment over this family line is over, and I forbid the generational spirit of addiction from going on to the children of the person for whom I am praying. I then pray over each troubling, addictive spirit afflicting the person and command it to leave.

Category F deals with collecting information on the background and cultural heritage of the person which can sometimes be useful. I personally know and understand many cultures, and this has come in handy a few times. Certain cultures have a tendency toward specific bondages.

1. What is your country of birth?

2. Have you lived in other countries? Which ones?

3. Where was your mother born (city, state, nation)? Your father (city, state, nation)?

4. Where were your grandparents born (city, state, nation)? Mother's mother? Mother's father? Father's mother? Father's father?

Category G is a miscellaneous section.

1. Do you suffer from any chronic illness or allergies? Is it hereditary?
Here we look for hereditary spirits of infirmity, as well as a specific spirit of infirmity. I always pray against a spirit of infirmity if there are allergies or chronic illness, and I pray for healing as well.

2. Have you had any severe accidents or traumas that stand out in your mind (not already mentioned above)?
If a spirit of trauma has not surfaced previously in the prayer time, but one turns up here, now is the time to pray against it.

3. Describe yourself in as many one- or two- word phrases as you can.

This is a helpful mirror of the person's self-image. Specific problems can turn up here that were missed previously. For example, if the word "lazy" shows up, I will pray against a spirit of sloth. I use this part for a final prayer to pray the opposite of negative perceptions the person has of himself or herself and ask God to help with those perceived problems, especially if they have to do with self-discipline or bad behavior.

4. Do you have any other problems you feel this questionnaire hasn't uncovered? Explain as fully as you can. Try to pinpoint when they began and if it was connected with a trauma of some sort, if you were victimized, or if you invited the problem in.

Note:

Much of this material is taken from the book *Evicting Demonic Intruders* by Noel and Phyl Gibson, published by New Wine Press. Distributed in the United States by Renew. Used by permission of the author.

EPILOGUE

does this stuff really work?

My husband, Peter, asked me to teach deliverance to certain classes of his students at Fuller Seminary. We began by using just an hour, then it expanded to a whole morning, and students seemed to want more depth in the teaching. We eventually incorporated a whole day of teaching into the 10-day intensive class on healing that he was teaching, both in the master's as well as the Doctor of Ministry level.

One day, as I finished teaching the Doctor of Ministry class, a dear pastor, who had never been exposed to such teaching (and quite possibly had been told in his ministerial training that we don't have demons here in our civilized country), asked a sincere question. His question is the title of this chapter—"Does this stuff really work?"

a pastor's letter

I had just received a letter a few days before and tucked it into my teaching notes for want of a better place to put it, so I tearfully read it to the class. I always get so touched when I read this letter. When I was done, there was complete silence for a few minutes while I wiped my eyes. The letter was from a pastor who would be a peer of the class I was teaching. Here is what it said:

> On March 18th, I came to your office to receive prayer in regard to some personal struggles and warfare. I'm writing back to let you know that God is doing a fantastic work! I don't even know where to begin. Let's just say that the problems with masturbation, anxiety, fear, and deceit are virtually gone. The magnitude of control, peace, power, and joy are overwhelming. I have never sensed such radical vision for ministry as I have since our time of prayer. God has truly blessed beyond my comprehension. Scriptures such as Deuteronomy 34:10, Psalm 33:1ff, esp. vv.15-18, Jeremiah 29:11-14a, and Acts 13:22 have come alive and penetrated my spiritual being to the very core. In a nutshell, I'm a new man for God.
>
> I know you won't take credit for what happened, and I know that it is God the Father who has His Spirit in full control. But, "Thank you, Doris." God has used you because you were willing to be obedient. God has opened the door to move into a Senior Pastorate, my baby girl was born healthy and strong on April 5th, my prayer life has risen to a new height. A keen sense of clarity has fallen on me in the areas of discernment, vision, equipping, evangelism, and leadership. May God continue to bless you and the ministry you have, as well as that of Peter.

> In closing, I would like to let you know that if you ever provide a conference, seminar, or workshop to help pastors with these areas, I would count it a privilege to share my testimony, intercede for the event, or come share in some helpful manner. Having gone through two disciplinary processes, the full weight of warfare involvement, and finally coming through it all to the Glory of God, I can't see how we (the church) can allow pastors and church leaders to fall victims to the enemy. A life is a very valuable investment in God's kingdom work. Once again, thank you.

That, dear friends, says it all. I personally would just like to add two things. First of all, the person doing the praying deserves none of the credit for anything good that happens. We are merely obedient conduits doing what we are commanded by the Lord. We are certainly nothing special at all.

The second observation is that the most thankful people on planet Earth are those set free from bondage. It is as though a person were let out of jail and stepped into a glorious flower garden on a sparkling, sunshiny day. To be an instrument in God's hand, to open up the jail door, is a privilege as well as a command. The example of Mary Magdalene in Scripture is precious to me. She was one of the Lord's most devoted followers after having been set free, and Jesus treated her accordingly—He loved her and honored her.

more sincere testimonies

I will share with you a few pages of testimonies you can expect to hear from grateful people. These are just a few quotes copied directly from letters I have kept in my file. As you will recall, I never keep questionnaires, just a few of the "thank you" letters that I feel the authors have no trouble with my keeping. I will share no names, but be assured that they are real letters from my file entitled "Deliverance Testimonies."

I will use these testimonies to respond to the Doctor of Ministry student: "Yes, Pastor, this stuff really does work!"

A Missionary to Asia

I thank God for the power of prayer and the time of deliverance. The cloud that was hanging over me has lifted. Like night to day. Praise the Lord!

A Woman from California

I am no longer suicidal, and I thank you more than words can express for your help at a time when everyone seemed to be denying me.

An Asian Seminary Student's Wife

I am experiencing a new kind of freedom that I never had before. I feel very lighthearted nowadays and take daily chores and happenings in life with a quiet assurance that God is always at hand to help me. Sometimes I'm surprised that I react to situations so differently from the past and wonder what's wrong with me. Then I realize it must be the transforming power of the Holy Spirit. I asked my husband if he saw any changes in me and he said, "Oh yes, tremendous changes. For a start, when you discipline the children, the strokes are controlled. You don't flare up easily. I see a great change in your personality."

I had been struggling with God for many years and often ended in frustration until God sent you.

A Woman from California

I hated my husband and had contacted an attorney to get a divorce. I became suicidal and was hospitalized. I had family problems. Then Doris prayed. The hate for my husband is gone. Every day I pray and look for ways to please him. The family is healing. Things turned around 180°. We are excited for each new day to see what God does.

(As we prayed, this woman told me about a severe financial need she had—it was a $5,000 tax bill from the IRS. After this woman prayed to forgive her husband, and we prayed for everything we could, we asked the Lord to miraculously supply this need. It was already the first week in April and the money was due the next week. She called me a couple of days after we prayed and said, "You'll never guess what happened. I was awakened at 7 A.M. by a phone call from the East Coast Disability Insurance office. I had applied for disability two years ago and never heard from them. The person on the other end of the phone said that my papers had literally fallen between a couple of desks and were just recovered. They are paying me for the back disability they owe—$5,000 is in the mail!" I think this is an excellent example of a broken bondage of hatred releasing a blessing.)

A Seminary Student's Paper for Another Class

From the minute I walked into Doris' office, I felt safe and confident that if there were any "critters" they would soon be gone. As a mother of three and grandmother to many, she has the uncanny ability to make you feel like her own child with a boo-boo on your knee coming inside for a bandage and a hug.... In three hours, my life was transformed by the power of the Holy Spirit. Praise be to God!!!

A Man from Oregon

I have experienced relief in every area we prayed about. As I left your office that day, I felt refreshed and prayed for, to be sure. A few days later, when faced with a situation that would have normally sent me down the tubes with depression, to my utter amazement I was able to pray right then and call it for what it was. I said aloud that I had been delivered from that once and for all. The feeling of doom and depression went away just like that! My life has taken a turn for the best enough so that my lovely wife of 21 years has noticed a real change in me.

A Seminary Graduate Student

I've got to tell you, it's a brand new world for me! I feel like, at last, I'm free and really alive. I can't get over it. Two things that seemed to bring the most healing for me was when you broke the spirit of false prophet and the spirit of self-rejection to which it was rooted. But when you gently showed me my resentment toward God—let me tell you what happened. The next morning in my prayer time, I began asking the Lord to show me if I had any more resentment toward Him that I hadn't dealt with. He showed me several things, and in the privacy of my apartment I was able to let repentance flow freely. I wept and wept in godly grief over my anger toward Him. The cleansing and subsequent infilling of God's Spirit was glorious. Since then my joy has been uncontainable.

A Woman from Ohio

I didn't understand until our time together what the total joy of the Lord was. Nor did I have any idea how strong I could feel in the Lord with total freedom. I literally feel as if a mighty "weight" has been lifted from my midriff. It is a very physical feeling and it is wonderful. Before our prayer time there were days when I fought such overwhelming fear that I would be living from minute to minute. At long last I feel He has positioned me for His Holiness. Finally being free from fear and guilt, He can begin to refine and purify all He's been about through this life of mine.

A Man from Central California

I am glad you gave me some post-prayer direction before leaving. Satan tried to enslave me the moment I walked out of your office. As I rebuked and kept rebuking, Satan left me alone. Things have been different since you prayed for me. I am a changed person. I feel free whereas once I felt bound. Most importantly, my relationship with my wife has improved dramatically. It is so much nicer to be able to give and receive love without pulling back. As I continue to pray God's healing of the memories related to my attempted suicide, the tightness is slowly leaving me.

A Hispanic Missionary from Florida

The Lord has answered our prayers, He heard our cries, and He delivered me from evil. We have been extensively traveling across the nation, and the Spirit of the Lord has met me at every place I preach and blessed us beyond imagination. At the time of my visit to your office my weight was just over 125 pounds, and now it's 142! Impossible!

A Pastor from Minnesota Attending a Deliverance Ministry Class at Fuller Seminary

I wanted to write this letter sooner because the change in my life has been so drastic. The morning after our meeting,

I remember waking up, and the strangest thing happened to me. For the first time in my life, that I can remember, my mind was at peace. It was as if someone had taken an eraser and had wiped clean all of the continual barrage of thoughts that assailed me.... For the first time it seems I am able to know what normal temptation is like. This might sound strange to you, but with the raging battles within being silenced, outward temptation is much more manageable, to say the least.... Our meeting has had profound theological ramifications as well. I believe we (the church) have looked upon deliverance ministries with much disdain. Deliverance isn't everything, but it must be embraced by the Church with much more respect. Far too many believers are suffering like I was.... It is good to be free, and I plan on staying this way. Thank you, Jesus, for the power of your work to set the captives free!

A Husband/Wife Pastoral Team from Massachusetts
Since our meeting with you, God has been more than merciful. My wife has had no self-destructive urges or desires and her sense of despair has considerably lessened. I have been free from the enslavement of unwanted thoughts, temptations, and urges in the sexual realm to a degree that I have not experienced since childhood. I have had far more self-control when dealing with frustrating situations. The instant flashes of anger and the bent toward a critical spirit are no longer automatic reactions. Now I feel that the Lord is truly far more in control of me, and that the blessings of discipline and self-control are far more evident in my life, Praise God! We are both very grateful for your help and the new freedom in Christ that we have both experienced.

A Young Woman from Los Angeles

My main purpose for prayer was a suicidal tendency. Whenever something went wrong or I got depressed, suicide was my first thought. This had been so since I can remember, maybe as young as 9 years old. For the first time in my life, suicide is not an option. Do you know that not even a thought of it enters my situation or mind?. . . All my life I had pornographic pictures in my mind and thoughts–not any more! Before there was a strange attraction, and for the first time I can recall, there is an actual repulsion. The last thing that happened is that I believe for the first time in my life I know what true love is. I realized that I loved this man, and he told me that he loves me and wants to marry me. He is the most wonderful man. All of this is beyond anything I would ever have imagined could be in my life. Thank you for your prayer.

A Secretary from a University in Los Angeles

I am amazed at how free of torment I feel now. A certain frightening and heavy oppression inside me is just simply gone now. I feel so new and renewed and liberated. God really restored my soul for me. It is something I haven't had since I was 8 or 12. It is so precious to me!

A Canadian Pastor

Here are a few entries from my journal since you prayed for me: I feel more emotionally mature. Mood swings have been reduced. I have been obtaining new freedom in the areas of unforgiveness, resentment, and bitterness, and I no longer feel consumed by it. Previous sleeplessness is gone, and there are no more bad dreams. My fear of dealing with people personally has disappeared. This I cannot understand, but accept gratefully. I have lost my fear of the future, and my fear of public speaking has significantly reduced. I actually look forward to preaching on Sunday mornings.

A Pastor in Orange County, California

Things are going better than I ever imagined possible. One of the things we prayed for was perceived rejection and fear of rejection. That seemed to be the "biggie" and grew out of my mother's death when I was six, and the dysfunction I grew up with (alcoholism and mental illness in my family). I now don't fear conflict and issues can be handled quickly and healthily. My relationships with my wife and children have also changed dramatically. My fear of rejection caused me to be a chronic achiever, and I could rarely relax and enjoy their company. Now we are all more at ease and can give and take direction from each other freely.

A Pastor in New Jersey

Your ministry of 2 hours and 45 minutes in a deliverance session was an outstanding blessing. I feel an enormous freedom that has blessed me personally, my wife, children, and the local church. My wife and I have grown closer as a couple. My children are more trusting of Daddy, and I don't feel the compulsive, uncontrollable anger. I already have two persons lined up for deliverance sessions with me, and there are more to come, I am sure. I have been wonderfully set free! I finally have a level playing field to grow in grace.

A Christian Worker in Colorado

The deliverance you administered has been thorough and complete. In my wife's words, it is as though I am a different man. Just the next day, my wife and I were sitting in Chili's restaurant and I noticed that the wandering eye had calmed down. I was not lusting after any woman there. With tears in my eyes, I shared this with her, and we both recognized the fruit of God's work. One thing so noticeable is the way temptations now come. Temptations came from inside before—as a driving force. Now any temptations that come are obviously sent from outside of me as an offering to see if I am interested. They are easier to resist. The deliverance has brought me a new level of strength to submit to God and resist the devil.

Someone from California Who Had Suffered Severe Trauma

It is amazing that some things come into one's life so noisily and dramatically, but leave so quietly. I wasn't aware of how deeply affected I was—thank you for your special gift.

A Pastor in New Hampshire

I feel like I have a whole new lease on life. I arose and had a time of praise and fellowship with Jesus in the Word. I feel free—like a huge burden has been lifted off of me. Thank you so much for what you did. I have hope again. I'm profoundly aware of the Lord's great mercy on me, and it makes me love Him more than ever.

appendices

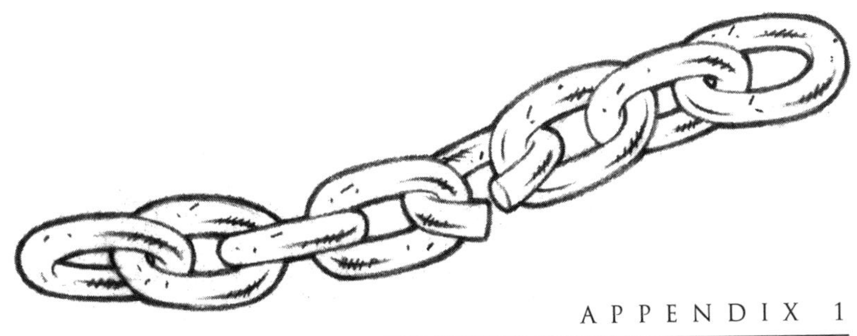

APPENDIX 1

form letter

Every questionnaire I give out is accompanied by a form letter from myself in which I inform the one requesting prayer of my requirements and expectations, and ask them to sign the bottom. Here is a sample of the form letter:

> This is a prayer ministry only. We are neither psychological nor medical professionals. We do not charge for our time. We request that you sign this instruction sheet, as well as the legal form that follows, stating that you are voluntarily requesting prayer and promise not to sue us for praying for you.
>
> Be prepared for an appointment that will last approximately two or more hours. Make note of incidents that produced trauma in your life and give a brief explanation of them as well.
>
> Full disclosure and honesty are a requirement. If an individual, living or dead, has been responsible for pain

or trauma in the present or past, you must be willing to pray to forgive that person, or results will not be satisfactory. If you are not willing to do this, please postpone your appointment and pray for the ability to do this. Wait until you are able, or at least willing, to forgive. Forgiveness is a choice, not a feeling. Submit your questionnaire and make an appointment at that time.

You may wish to fast on the day of your appointment. If you have friends who know you are coming, you may wish to ask them to fast and pray for us, if you would be comfortable doing that. Neither of these is a requirement, but it usually helps.

You must promise to break with willful sin and bad habits and really desire to get rid of demonic bondages in order for us to make an appointment.

Before we begin our session, you may be asked to pray the following prayer aloud (it may be read):

I confess Jesus Christ to be my personal Savior.

I renounce any oppression from the evil one in my life because of iniquity, transgression, and sin of my parents, ancestors or myself and humbly ask God for release and cleansing through the blood of Jesus Christ.

I repent from every sinful attitude, action or habit of mine which does not glorify Jesus Christ and ask forgiveness, release, cleansing and wholeness.

I renounce the devil and all demonic influences, bondages, dominations and infirmities in my life.

I ask You, Lord, for the release and freedom promised by Jesus Christ so that He may be Lord of my total personality and be glorified in all I say and do. In His name I pray, amen.

This must be your honest and sincere desire, or we will need to postpone ministry until a later time.

When your form is completed, please return it at least 10 days before your scheduled appointment. If you are unable to keep your appointment, please phone ______________ at least 24 hours in advance.

I have read these instructions, understand them, and agree to comply fully.

(Signature)

____

(Date)

____

Print name, address and phone number:

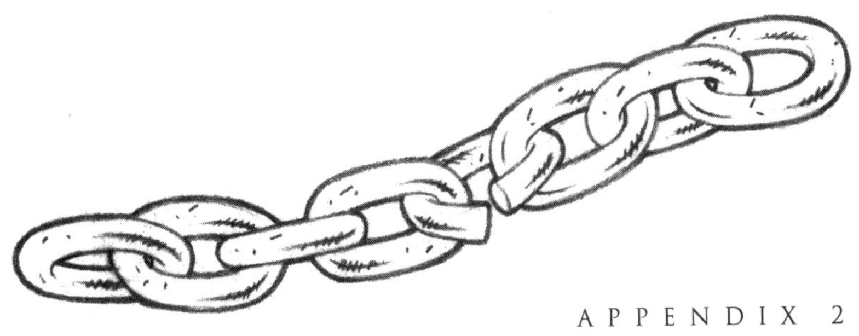

APPENDIX 2

legal waiver

I ask everyone requesting prayer to sign a legal waiver. My lawyer drew up this document, and it may or may not be useful to you. I am requesting that if you use this document, please check it over with a lawyer from your state (or nation) to see if any corrections or additions need to be made. Please do not use it unless you have it reviewed. It may be submitted to your lawyer as a sample for guidance if it is useful to him or her.

voluntary release, assumption of risk and indemnity agreement

In consideration for being permitted to participate in voluntary prayer ministry, herein referred to as the "Prayer Ministry," the undersigned, ______________________________, herein referred to as the "Releaser," agrees as follows:

1. **RELEASE, WAIVER, DISCHARGE AND COVENANT NOT TO SUE.** Releaser and Releaser's personal representatives, assigns, insurer, heirs, executors, administrators, spouse and next of kin, hereby releases, waives, discharges and covenants not to sue______________________________,
located at ____,
and its directors, officers, employees, agents, volunteers as well as it successors, assigns, affiliates, subordinates, and subsidiaries, all herein referred to as the "Releasees," from any and all liability to Releaser, and to Releaser's personal representatives, assigns, insurer, heirs, executors, administrators, spouses and next of kin for any and all loss, damage, or cost on account of injury to the person or property or resulting in the death of Releaser, whether caused by the negligence of Releasees or otherwise while Releaser is participating in the Prayer Ministry and any other activities in connection with the Prayer Ministry.

2. **ASSUMPTION OF RISK.** Releaser understands, is aware of, and assumes all risks inherent in participating in the Prayer Ministry. These risks include, but are not limited to, physical and emotional responses and reactions as a result of this prayer ministry.

3. **INDEMNITY.** Releaser agrees to indemnify Releasees from any liability, loss, damage or cost Releasees may incur due to the participation by Releaser in the Prayer Ministry whether caused by the negligence of Releasees or otherwise. Releaser assumes full responsibility for and risk of bodily injury, death or property damage due to negligence of Releasees or otherwise while participating in the Prayer Ministry.

Releaser expressly agrees that this Voluntary Release, Assumption of Risk and Indemnity agreement, herein referred to as "Agreement," is intended to be as broad and inclusive as permitted by the laws of the State of ______________________________ and that, if any portion of this Agreement is held invalid, it is agreed that a balance, notwithstanding, continue in full legal force and effect. This Agreement contains the entire agreement between the parties in regard to the Prayer Ministry.

RELEASER REPRESENTS THAT:

I HAVE CAREFULLY READ THIS AGREEMENT. I UNDERSTAND IT IS A RELEASE OF ALL CLAIMS, INCLUDING THE NEGLIGENCE OF RELEASEES.

I UNDERSTAND THAT I ASSUME ALL RISKS INHERENT IN THE PRAYER MINISTRY SET FORTH IN THIS AGREEMENT.

I UNDERSTAND THAT I AM INDEMNIFYING THE RELEASEES.

I VOLUNTARILY SIGN MY NAME EVIDENCING MY UNDERSTANDING AND ACCEPTANCE OF THE PROVISIONS OF THIS AGREEMENT.

Signature of Releaser:

____ Date________________

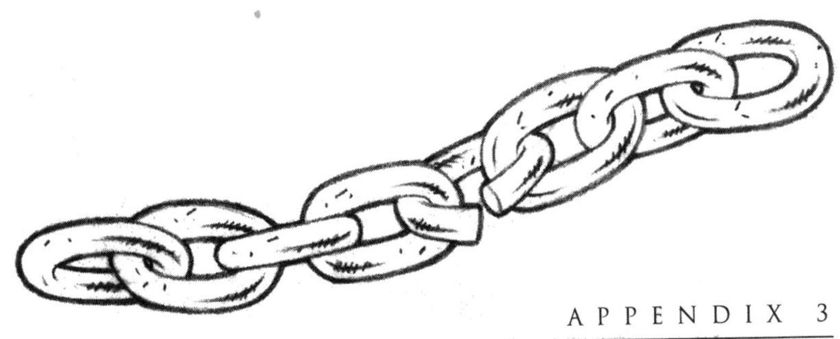

APPENDIX 3

the questionnaire

The following is the ministry questionnaire outlined in chapters 9 through 14.

This document has been modified from material in *Evicting Demonic Intruders* by Noel and Phyl Gibson (Ventura, CA: Renew Books, 1993) and is used by permission. It is recommended that these pages be enlarged when copying to provide more space for answering questions.

The questionnaire may not be copied for sale at any time, but it is reproducible for noncommercial use.

Name: ____

Age:______________

Marital Status:

single married divorced remarried widowed

Current profession:

____

Please answer the following briefly:

1. What is your church background?

2. Explain briefly your conversion experience. If you came to Christ as a teenager or older, was your life really changed?

3. Were you baptized as a child? yes no
   Were you baptized as a convert? yes no

4. In one word, who is Jesus Christ to you?

5. What does the blood of Calvary mean to you?

6. Is repentance part of your Christian life?

7. What is your prayer life like?

8. Do you have assurance of salvation?

9. Do you have a problem with doubt and unbelief in everyday Christian living?

10. Are you satisfied with your Christian walk? yes no
    If not, how would you like to see it improve?

CATEGORY A (CIRCLE ALL ANSWERS THAT APPLY)

1. Was your relationship with your parents? (circle one)
   good bad indifferent
   Explain:
   a. Any special problems with your father?
   b. With your mother?
   c. With your brother(s) or sister(s)?

2. a. Were you a planned child? yes no don't know
   b. The "right" sex? yes no don't know
   c. Were you conceived out of wedlock?
      yes no don't know
   d. Were you adopted? yes no don't know
   e. If adopted, do you know anything about your natural parents?

f. Do you know if your mother suffered any trauma during her pregnancy with you?

g Did you have a difficult or complicated birth?

h. Were you "bonded at birth"? yes no don't know
A breast-fed baby? yes no don't know

i. Do you have brothers and sisters?

Name: ______________________ Age:________

Name: ______________________ Age:________

Name: ______________________ Age:________

Where do you fall in the sibling line?

How was your relationship with them growing up?

What is it like now?

Any special problems?

3. Are your parents living?
Father? yes no
Mother? yes no
Are they Christians?
Father? yes no
Mother? yes no
Living together? yes no
Divorced? yes no
How old were you when they were divorced? ________

Remarried?

Father yes no

Mother yes no

How is your relationship with stepparents?

Are they Christians?

Stepbrothers? Stepsisters?

How was your relationship growing up?

How is your relationship now?

4. Are you a critical person? yes no maybe
5. Do you feel emotionally immature?

   yes no not necessarily
6. Tell us about your self-image (circle all applicable):

   low self-image
   condemn myself
   feel worthless
   feel inferior
   punish myself
   (if so, how?)
   feel insecure
   hate myself
   believe I am a failure
   question my identity

7. What was your father like? (circle one)

   passive strong and manipulative neither

   Were you friends? yes no sort of

   Discribe briefly your relationship with your father:

8. What was your mother like? (circle one)
   passive strong and manipulative neither
   Were you friends? yes no sort of
   Describe briefly your relationship with your mother:

9. Was yours a happy home during childhood?
   Describe briefly:

10. How would you describe your family's financial situation when you were a child?
    poor slight financial struggles
    moderate income affluent

11. Has lying or stealing been a problem to you? yes no
    Is it now? yes no

12. Were you lonely as a teenager? yes sometimes never
    Explain:

13. As a child, teenager, or later in life did you ever suffer an injustice? What?

    By whom?

14. Do you have trouble giving or receiving love?
    yes no at times

15. Do you find it easy to communicate with persons close to you?
    I have real difficulty
    I am unwilling
    I have some problems at times
    It's easy

16. Are you a perfectionist? yes no
    Were (are) your parents perfectionists? yes no

17. Do you come from a proud family? yes no

18. Do you personally have a problem with pride? yes no

19. Do you have or have you had problems with (circle all applicable):

impatience	irritability
temper	racial prejudice
moodiness	rebellion
violence	stubbornness
anger	temptation to murder

20. Have you been given to:
    Swearing? Blasphemies? Obscenities?
    Do you now:
    Swear? Blaspheme? Use obscenities?

21. Do you have the following feelings toward anyone:
Unforgiveness? Whom and why?

Resentment? Whom and why?

Bitterness? Whom and why?

Hatred? Whom and why?

CATEGORY B

1. Are you easily frustrated? yes no
Do you show it or bury it? show bury

2. Are you an anxious person? Worrier? Get depressed?

3. Did either of your parents suffer from depression?
no father mother

4. Has any parent, brother or sister, grandparent suffered from an acute nervousness or mental problem?
yes no
Whom?
Problem?

5. Have you personally ever had psychiatric counseling?
   yes no
   Hospitalization? yes no
   Shock treatment? yes no
   Psychoanalysis? yes no
   Other? yes no

6. Have you ever been hypnotized? yes no
   If so, when and why?

7. Have you had advanced education? yes no
   If so, what?

8. Have you, your parents or grandparents been in any cults (circle all applicable):

   Christian Science
   Bahai
   gurus
   Unity
   Spiritist churches
   Christadelphians
   Theosophy
   Mormons
   Eastern religions such as Hinduism, Buddhism (Zen, Tibetan), etc.
   Rosicrucian
   Jehovah's Witnesses
   Native religions
   Unification Church (Moonies)
   Children of Love
   Scientology
   religious communes
   Islam

   Other:

9. To your knowledge, has any close family member been a(n):

Freemason	Oddfellow
Rainbow Girl	Mormon
Eastern Star	Shriner
Daughter of the Nile	Job's Daughter
Elk	De Molay

If so, whom?

Do you suffer from (circle where applicable):

apathy	confusion
hardness of emotion	financial disaster
skepticism	doubt
unbelief	allergies
infirmities	frequent sickness
mockery	comprehension difficulties

Is there any Masonic regalia or memorabilia in your possession? yes no

If so, what?

10. Do you feel mentally confused? yes no
    Have mental blocks? yes no
11. Do you daydream? yes no
    Have mental fantasies? yes no
12. Do you suffer from frequent bad dreams? yes no
    Sleeplessness? yes no
13. Have you ever been tempted to commit suicide?
    yes no
    If yes, when and why?

Have you tried? yes no

If yes, how, when and why?

14. Have you ever wished to die? yes no

Spoken it aloud? yes no

15. Have you had a strong and prolonged fear of any of the following:

failure
inadequacy
the dark
rape
being alone
the future
crowds
men
public speaking
the opinion of people
death or injury of a loved one
divorce or marriage
insects
dogs
animals
pain
flying in an airplane
grocery stores
inability to cope
authority figures
death
violence
Satan and evil spirits
women
heights
insanity
accident
old age
enclosed places
terminal illness
breakup
spiders
snakes
water
loud noises
open spaces

Since becoming a Christian, do any of the above fears still grip you? yes no

If so, which ones?

CATEGORY C

1. Have you ever made a pact with the devil? yes no
   Was it a blood pact?

   What was it?

   When?

   Why?

   Are you willing to renounce it? yes no

2. To your knowledge, has any curse been placed on you or your family? yes no
   By whom?

   Why?

   Explain:

3. To your knowledge, have your parents or any relative as far back as you know been involved in occultism or witchcraft? yes no
   Whom and doing what?

   To what extent?

4. Have you ever had involvement with any of the following:

fortune tellers	tarot cards
Ouija boards	séances
mediums	palmistry
astrology	color therapy
levitation	astral travel
horoscope	lucky charms
black magic	demon worship
asked for a spirit guide	clairvoyance
crystals	done automatic handwriting
New Age movement	been to a curandero or native healer

Been involved in any other witchcraft or demonic or satanic things? If so, what?

5. Have you ever read books on occultism or witchcraft?
   yes no
   Why?

6. Have you played demonic games such as Dungeons & Dragons? yes no
   Watched demonic films? yes no
   Do you now? yes no
7. Have you been involved in transcendental meditation?
   yes no
   Do you have a mantra? yes no
   If so, what is it?

8. Have you been involved in Eastern religions? yes no
   Followed a guru? yes no

9. Have you ever visited heathen temples? yes no
   When?
   Made offerings? yes no
   What were they?

   Did you take part in any ceremony?
   Explain:

10. Have you ever done any form of yoga? yes no
    Meditation? yes no
    Exercises? yes no

11. Have you ever learned or used any form of mind communication or mind control? yes no
    Explain:

12. Were your parents or grandparents superstitious?
    yes no
    Were or are you? yes no

13. Have you ever worn lucky charms, fetishes, amulets, or signs of the zodiac? yes no

    Do you have any in your possession? yes no

14. Do you have in your home any symbols of idols or spirit worship, such as:

Buddhas	totem poles
painted face masks	idol carvings
fetish objects or feathers	pagan symbols
tikis	kachina dolls
native art (if so what?)	other?

Where are they from, and how did you get them?

15. Do you have any witches, such as "good-luck kitchen witches," in your home?

16. Are you "turned on" by any of the following music:

rock and roll	punk rock
New Age	rap
heavy metal	

How much time do you spend listening to it?

17. Have you ever learned any of the martial arts?
yes no
If so, which?

Do you practice it now?

18. Have you ever had premonitions? yes no
Déjà vu? yes no
Psychic sight? yes no

19. Have you ever been involved in firewalking?
    Voodoo?
    Any other form of pagan religious ceremony?
    If so, what and when?

20. Do you have any tattoos? yes no
    If so, of what?

CATEGORY D

1. Do you have lustful thoughts? yes no
   Of what?

   Frequency?

2. To your knowledge, was there evidence of lust in your parents, grandparents or further back? yes no
   Explain:

3. Do you frequently masturbate? yes no
   How often?
   Do you know why?

   Do you feel it is a compulsive problem? yes no

4. Were you ever sexually molested by someone outside your family as a child or teenager? yes no
   By whom?
   More than once?
   Explain:

   Were you actually raped?
   By whom?
   More than once?
   Explain:

5. Have you ever been a victim of incest by a family member?
   yes no
   Whom?
   Often?
   Extended period?

6. **Men:** Have you ever molested or raped anyone?
   yes no
   Names:
   Committed incest? yes no

   Women: Have you ever been raped? yes no
   Names:
   Explain:

7. Have you ever committed fornication (single persons)?
yes no
How many partners?
First names and when?

With prostitutes? How many?
When?

Others?

Have you ever committed adultery (at least one partner married)? yes no
First name(s) and when:

Are you currently involved in an illicit sexual relationship? yes no
Name:
Are you willing to break it off? yes no

8. Have you ever had homosexual or lesbian desires?
yes no
Do you now? yes no
Experience? yes no
Whom and when?

9. (married women only) Are you sexually frigid? yes no

10. Have you ever sexually fantasized about an animal?
yes no
Committed a sex act (bestiality) with an animal?
yes no
Name all animals involved:

11. Has pornography ever attracted you? yes no
How did you become involved?

Names of persons involved.

To what extent?

Is it still a problem? yes no
Have you seen porn movies? yes no
Videos? yes no
Live sex shows? yes no
Do you currently purchase or rent porn or have such a channel on your home TV? yes no
Do you look at Internet porn? yes no

12. Have you ever been involved in oral sex? yes no
With whom?

13. Have you been involved in anal sex? yes no
    With whom?

14. **Women:** Have you ever had an abortion? yes no
    How many?
    Give dates and name (s) of father(s):

    Men: Have you ever fathered a child that was forcefully aborted? yes no
    How many? When?
    Give dates and name(s) of mother(s):

15. Have you been plagued with desires of having sex with a child (pedophilia)?
    yes no
    Have you actually done so? yes no
16. Have you ever had inner sexual stimulation and climax out of your control, especially at night? By this I mean, do you have dreams of a personage approaching and asking to have sex with you, or just doing it, and you "feel" a presence in bed with you and then wake up with a sexual climax? (This is something other than a normal nocturnal emission.) yes no
17. Have you ever gone to a massage parlor and been sexually stimulated? yes no

18. How would you describe your sexual relationship with your spouse?

CATEGORY E

1. Did any of your family as far back as you know have addictions of any kind?
   yes no To what?

2. Have you ever been addicted to any of the following:
   Alcohol? yes no
   Smoking? yes no
   Food? yes no
   Gambling? yes no
   Compulsive exercise? yes no
   Being a spendthrift? yes no
   Watching TV? yes no
   Coffee? yes no
   Drugs (prescribed or hallucinatory)? yes no
   Which ones?
   Are any of the above a current problem?

CATEGORY F

1. What is your country of birth?

2. Have you lived in other countries? yes no
   Which ones?

3. Where was your mother born? (city, state, nation)

   Your father? (city, state, nation)

4. Where were your grandparents born? (city, state, nation)
   Mother's mother?
   Mother's father?
   Father's mother?
   Father's father?

CATEGORY G

1. Do you suffer from any chronic illness or allergies? yes no
   Which ones?

   Is it hereditary?

2. Have you had any severe accidents or traumas that stand out in your mind (not already mentioned above)?
   Explain:

3. Describe yourself in as many one- or two-word phrases as you can:

a.	h.
b.	i.
c.	j.
d.	k.
e.	l.
f.	m.
g.	n.

4. Do you have any other problems you feel this questionnaire hasn't uncovered? (Explain as fully as you can. Try to pinpoint when they began and if each was connected with a trauma of some sort, if you were victimized, or if you invited the problem in.

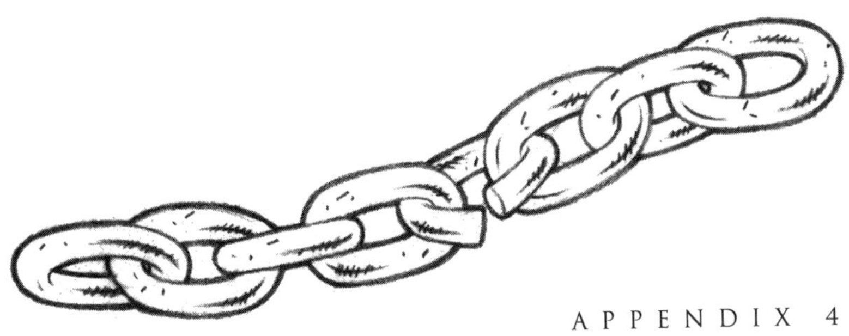

APPENDIX 4

post-prayer instructions

The following instructions are used from Noel and Phyl Gibson's *Freedom in Christ* (Chichester, England: New Wine Press, 1996), pages 189-192, and are used with permission. The material has been slightly adapted with appropriate scriptural inserts and minor editing.

After I finish praying for the person and spending some time giving a few verbal post-prayer instructions, I give the person this wonderful printed set of Post-Prayer Instructions done by Noel and Phyl Gibson. It is so good for them to have these in their Bibles and review them often the first days and weeks after the deliverance session.

post-prayer instructions

Freedom in Christ is God's love gift to you at the cost of the lifeblood of His beloved Son. It needs to be guarded carefully and worked out diligently in daily living.

The ministry of freedom is the working of the grace of God in your life by the Holy Spirit. From now on, He relies on your active cooperation:

- To recover full use of functions the devil has restricted
- To exercise the lordship of Christ in areas previously used by the evil one for his purposes
- To help you reach fulfillment where before you experienced frustration and disappointment
- To return you to victories you once knew or to lift you to new levels of spiritual understanding and usefulness for the glory of Jesus Christ

Just as the step of faith in Jesus Christ for salvation led to a commitment of discipleship, so the ministry of freedom must be followed by commitment to a plan of spiritual rehabilitation. Works must always follow true faith.

The following steps are suggested for daily use to help you "work out your salvation" (Phil. 2:12,13).

sixteen principles for freedom in Christ

1. Confess the general areas in which you have received freedom positively and gratefully in prayer. *Don't allow one negative thought germinating space.*

   Principle: "that if you confess with your mouth the Lord Jesus and believe in your heart that God has raised Him from the dead, you will be saved. For with the heart one believes unto righteousness, and with the mouth confession is made unto salvation" (Rom. 10:9,10).

2. Meet each new day trusting in God's power to help you *make right choices.* Don't let your feelings deceive you.

   Principle: "Having begun in the Spirit, are you now being made perfect by the flesh?" (Gal. 3:3).

3. Expect continuous and increasing freedom where Satan has previously bound you or used you for his purposes. Move forward by faith *without even a glance over your shoulder at what is now past.*

   Principle: "Brethren, I do not count myself to have apprehended; but one thing I do, forgetting those things which are behind and reaching forward to those things which are ahead, I press toward the goal for the prize of the upward call of God in Christ Jesus" (Phil. 3:13,14).

4. Remember, anything the devil whispers in your ear is a lie. That's his profession and he's very good at it. John 8:44 says, "When he speaks a lie, he speaks from his own resources, for he is a liar and the father of it." If he tries to convince you that your freedom didn't really happen but was just in your mind or was emotional, *use your faith shield against him* and tell what God does to liars. He will soon give up.

   Principle: "Therefore submit to God. Resist the devil and he will flee from you. Draw near to God and He will draw near to you. Cleanse your hands, you sinners; and purify your hearts, you double-minded" (Jas. 4:7,8).

5. Don't hesitate to use the name of Jesus, the blood of the Lamb and your confession of faith against all Satan's temptations and condemnation. *All condemnation comes from Satan.* Never believe him. You have been blood cleansed and are blood protected.

   Principle: "And they overcame him by the blood of the Lamb and by the word of their testimony, and they did not love their lives to the death" (Rev. 12:11). "There is therefore now no condemnation to those who are in Christ Jesus, who do not walk according to the flesh, but according to the Spirit" (Rom. 8:1).

6. Avoid deliberate sin—like the plague.

   Principle: "We know that whoever is born of God does not sin; but he who has been born of God keeps himself, and the wicked one does not touch him" (1 John 5:18). Should you *unavoidably* sin, confess it immediately and receive forgiveness and *cleansing.* This will stop Satan from weighing you down with guilt, one of his favorite habits.

   Principle: "If we confess our sins, He is faithful and just to forgive us our sins and to cleanse us from all unrighteousness" (1 John 1:9).

7. *Rely upon the Holy Spirit* to control your life, your emotions, your desires and your imaginations, together with your will, by deliberately giving Christ's lordship over them each day.

   Principle: "I beseech you therefore, brethren, by the mercies of God, that you present your bodies a living sacrifice, holy, acceptable to God, which is your reasonable service. And do not be conformed to this world, but be transformed by the renewing of your mind, that you may prove what is that good and acceptable and perfect will of God (Rom. 12:1,2); "And do not be drunk with wine, in which is dissipation; but be filled with the Spirit," (Eph. 5:18); "Therefore He who supplies the Spirit to you and works miracles among you, does He do it by the works of the law, or by the hearing of faith?" (Gal. 3:5).

8. Take time or make time to read—learn—*meditate on God's Word every day.* If time is limited, carry Scripture verse cards with you for your free times.

   Principle: "This Book of the Law shall not depart from your mouth, but you shall meditate in it day and night, that you may observe to do according to all that is written in it. For then you will make your way prosperous, and then you will have good success" (Josh. 1:8); "Let the word of Christ dwell in you richly in all wisdom, teaching and admonishing one another in psalms and hymns and spiritual songs, singing with grace in your hearts to the Lord" (Col. 3:16).

9. Wear the armor of spiritual warfare *every day.* Put on each piece thoughtfully and prayerfully and be protected at all times. Don't forget the seventh piece is "prayer."

   Principle: "Finally, my brethren, be strong in the Lord and in the power of His might. Put on the whole armor of God, that you may be able to stand against the wiles of the devil. For we do not wrestle against flesh and blood, but against principalities, against powers, against the rulers of the darkness of this age, against spiritual hosts of wickedness in the heavenly places. Therefore take up the whole armor of God, that you may be able to withstand in the evil day, and having done all, to stand. Stand therefore, having girded your waist with truth, having put on the breastplate of righteousness, and having shod your feet with the preparation of the gospel of peace; above all, taking the shield of faith with which you will be able to quench all the fiery darts of the wicked one. And take the helmet of salvation, and the sword of the Spirit, which is the word of God; praying always with all prayer and supplication in the Spirit, being watchful to this end with all perseverance and supplication for all the saints" (Eph. 6:10-18).

10. *Keep your eyes and ears open* for all the sneaky traps the devil will leave around for you. Then "holler for help" to your heavenly Father, and He will immediately answer and give you the victory.

    Principle: "Therefore submit to God. Resist the devil and he will flee from you. Draw near to God and He will draw near to you. Cleanse your hands, you sinners; and purify your hearts, you double-minded" (Jas. 4:7,8).

11. *Concentrate* your thoughts and plans on what glorifies Christ and you will have victories all the time.

    Principle: "If then you were raised with Christ, seek those things which are above, where Christ is, sitting at the right hand of God. Set your mind on things above, not on things on the earth. For you died, and your life is hidden with Christ in God" (Col. 3:1-3).

12. *Beware of thinking you can make it alone.* You never will make it alone in life because God never intended you should. Be smart: admit you can't do it all by yourself, and then do things with His help.

Principle: "I am the vine, you are the branches. He who abides in Me, and I in him, bears much fruit; for without Me you can do nothing" (Heb. 13:5). "Let your conduct be without covetousness; be content with such things as you have. For He Himself has said, 'I will never leave you nor forsake you'" (John 15:5).

13. *Break wrong friendships* and choose positive, clean-living friends who put Jesus first.

    Principle: "Do you not know that friendship with the world is enmity with God? Whoever therefore wants to be a friend of the world makes himself an enemy of God" (Jas 4:4). Break former habits that led to sin. AVOID magazines, movies and television programs that you should not see.
    Principle: "Finally, brethren, whatever things are true, whatever things are noble, whatever things are just, whatever things are pure, whatever things are lovely, whatever things are of good report, if there is any virtue and if there is anything praiseworthy—meditate on these things" (Phil. 4:8).

14. *Never let up on warring against the list of no-nos.* Criticism, negativity, grieving over the past, oversensitivity, doubt, selfishness, putting feelings before faith, and prayerlessness are all on the list. Be an outgoing person and help others.

    Principle: "Now the works of the flesh are evident, which are: adultery, fornication, uncleanness, lewdness, idolatry, sorcery, hatred, contentions, jealousies, outbursts of wrath, selfish ambitions, dissensions, heresies, envy, murders, drunkenness, revelries, and the like; of which I tell you beforehand, just as I also told you in time past, that those who practice such things will not inherit the kingdom of God. Let us not become conceited, provoking one another, envying one another" (Gal. 5:19-21,26).

15. *Be a praising, thankful person,* always giving thanks to God for His continuous goodness.

    Principle: Psalm 103:6, "The LORD executes righteousness and justice for all who are oppressed."

16. *Finally, breathe* in by faith any of your nine personality needs supplied liberally by the Spirit of God from the glory of Jesus Christ at the right hand of His Father, who is also your Father.

    Principle: "But the fruit of the Spirit is love, joy, peace, longsuffering, kindness, goodness, faithfulness, gentleness, self-control. Against such there is no law" (Gal. 5:22,23). "So Jesus said to them again, 'Peace to you! As the Father has sent Me, I also send you'" (John 20:21).

Submission to the lordship of Christ and obedience to His will through His Word is essential to maintain freedom.

Then it will be as though I had sprinkled clean water on you, for you will be clean—your filthiness will be washed away, your idol worship gone. And I will give you a new heart—I will give you new and right desires—and put a new spirit within you. I will take out your stony heart of sin and give you new hearts of love. And I will put my spirit within you so that you will obey my laws and do whatever I command (Ezek. 36:25-27, *TLB*).

God bless you!

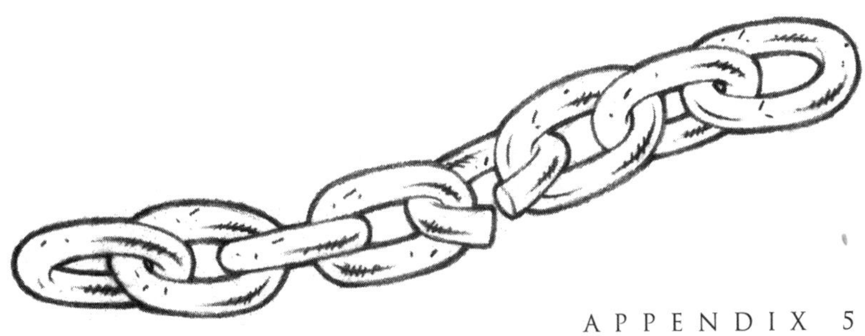

APPENDIX 5

prayer of release for freemasons and their descendants

The following material is used with permission of Selwyn Stevens and Jubilee Ministries in New Zealand. The prayer appears as it was originally written with the exception that a few words were altered to reflect Americanized spelling.

This prayer may not be copied for sale at any time, but it is reproducible for noncommercial use.

If you were once a member of a Masonic organization or are a descendant of someone who was, we recommend that you pray through this prayer from your heart. Please don't be like the Masons who are given their obligations and oaths one line at a time and without prior knowledge of the requirements. Please read it through first so you know what is involved. It is best to pray this aloud with a Christian witness present. We suggest a brief pause following each paragraph to allow the Holy Spirit to show any related issues which may require attention.

A significant number of people also reported having experienced physical and spiritual healings as diverse as long-term headaches and epilepsy as the result of praying through this prayer. Christian counselors and pastors in many countries have been using this prayer in counseling situations and seminars for several years, with real and significant results.

There are differences between British Commonwealth Masonry and American and Prince Hall Masonry in the higher degrees. *Degrees unique to Americans are marked with three stars at the beginning of each paragraph.* Those of British and Commonwealth descent shouldn't need to pray through those paragraphs.

Father God,
creator of heaven and earth,
I come to you in the name of Jesus Christ your Son.
I come as a sinner seeking forgiveness and cleansing from all sins
committed against you, and others made in your image.
I honor my earthly father and mother and all of my ancestors
of flesh and blood, and of the spirit by adoption and godpar-
ents, but I utterly turn away from
and renounce all their sins.
I forgive all my ancestors for the effects of their sins
on me and my children.

I confess and renounce all of my own sins.
I renounce and rebuke Satan and every spiritual power
of his affecting me and my family.

I renounce and forsake all involvement in Freemasonry or
any other lodge or craft by my ancestors and myself.
In the name of Jesus Christ,
I renounce and cut off Witchcraft, the principal
spirit behind Freemasonry,
and I renounce and cut off Baphomet, the Spirit of Antichrist
and the spirits of Death, and Deception.
I renounce the insecurity, the love of position and power,
the love of money, avarice or greed,
and the pride which would have led my
ancestors into Masonry.
I renounce all the fears which held them in Masonry,
especially the fears of death, fears of men, and fears of trusting,
in the name of Jesus Christ.

I renounce every position held in the lodge by any of
my ancestors or myself, including "Master,"
"Worshipful Master," or any other
I renounce the calling of any man "Master," for
Jesus Christ is my only master and Lord, and He
forbids anyone else having that title.
I renounce the entrapping of others into Masonry,
and observing the helplessness of others during the rituals.
I renounce the effects of Masonry passed on to me through
any female ancestor who felt distrusted and rejected by her
husband as he entered and attended any lodge and refused
to tell her of his secret activities.
I also renounce all obligations, oaths and curses enacted by

every female member of my family through any direct membership of all Women's Orders of Freemasonry, the Order of the Eastern Star, or any other Masonic or occultic organization.

33RD AND SUPREME DEGREE

In the name of Jesus Christ
I renounce the oaths taken and the curses involved in the supreme Thirty-Third Degree of Freemasonry, the Grand Sovereign Inspector General.
I renounce the secret passwords,
DEMOLAY-HIRUM ABIFF, FREDERICK OF PRUSSIA, MICHA, MACHA, BEALIM, and ADONAI
and all they mean.
I renounce all of the obligations of every Masonic degree, and all penalties invoked.

I renounce and utterly forsake
The Great Architect Of The Universe,
who is revealed in this degree as Lucifer,
and his false claim to be the universal fatherhood of God.
I renounce the cable-tow around the neck.
I renounce the death wish that the wine drunk from a human skull should turn to poison and the skeleton whose cold arms are invited if the oath of this degree is violated.

I renounce the three infamous assassins of their grand master, law, property and religion, and the greed and witchcraft involved in the attempt to manipulate and control the rest of mankind.

In the name of God the Father, Jesus Christ the Son,
and the Holy Spirit,
I renounce and break the curses involved in the idolatry, blasphemy, secrecy and deception of Freemasonry at every level, and I appropriate the Blood of Jesus Christ to cleanse all the consequences of these from my life. I now revoke all previous consent given by any of my ancestors or myself to be deceived.

BLUE LODGE

In the name of Jesus Christ
I renounce the oaths taken and the curses involved in the First or Entered Apprentice Degree, especially their effects on the throat and tongue.
I renounce the Hoodwink blindfold and its effects on spirit, emotions and eyes, including all confusion, fear of the dark, fear of the light, and fear of sudden noises.
I renounce the blinding of spiritual truth, the darkness of the soul, the false imagination, condescension and the spirit of poverty caused by the ritual of this degree.
I also renounce the usurping of the marriage covenant by the removal of the wedding ring.
I renounce the secret word, BOAZ, and all it means.
I renounce the serpent clasp on the apron, and the spirit of Python which it brought to squeeze the spiritual life out of me. I renounce the ancient pagan teaching from Babylon and Egypt and the symbolism of the First Tracing Board.

I renounce the mixing and mingling of truth and error,
the mythology, fabrications and lies taught as truth,
and the dishonesty by leaders as to the true
understanding of the ritual,
and the blasphemy of this degree of Freemasonry.
I renounce the presentation to every compass direction,
for all the Earth is the Lord's, and everything in it.

I renounce the cabletow noose around the neck,
the fear of choking
and also every spirit causing asthma, hay fever,
emphysema or any other breathing difficulty.
I renounce the ritual dagger, or the compass point, sword or
spear held against the breast, the fear of death by stabbing pain,
and the fear of heart attack from this degree, and the absolute
secrecy demanded under a witchcraft oath
and sealed by kissing the Volume of the Sacred Law.
I also renounce kneeling to the false deity
known as the Great Architect of the Universe, and humbly ask
the One True God to forgive me for this idolatry,
in the name of Jesus Christ.
I renounce the pride of proven character and good standing
required prior to joining Freemasonry,
and the resulting self-righteousness of being good enough
to stand before God without the need of a savior.
I now pray for healing of...
(throat, vocal cords, nasal passages, sinus, bronchial tubes, etc.)
for healing of the speech area,
and the release of the Word of God to me and through
me and my family.

In the name of Jesus Christ
I renounce the oaths taken and the curses
involved in the Second or Fellow Craft Degree of Masonry,
especially the curses on the heart and chest.
I renounce the secret words SHIBBOLETH and JACHIN,
and all that these mean.
I renounce the ancient pagan teaching and symbolism
of the Second Tracing Board.
I renounce the Sign of Reverence to the Generative Principle.
I cut off emotional hardness, apathy, indifference, unbelief,
and deep anger from me and my family.
In the name of Jesus Christ I pray for the healing of...
(the chest/lung/heart area) and also for the healing of my emotions, and ask to be made sensitive to the Holy Spirit of God.

In the name of Jesus Christ
I renounce the oaths taken and the curses
involved in the Third or Master Mason Degree,
especially the curses on the stomach and womb area.
I renounce the secret words TUBAL CAIN
and MAHA BONE, and all that they mean.
I renounce the ancient pagan teaching and symbolism
of the Third Tracing Board used in the ritual.
I renounce the Spirit of Death from the blows to the head
enacted as ritual murder, the fear of death, false martyrdom,
fear of violent gang attack, assault, or rape, and the
helplessness of this degree.
I renounce the falling into the coffin
or stretcher involved in the ritual of murder.

In the name of Jesus Christ
I renounce Hiram Abiff, the false savior of Freemasons

revealed in this degree.
I renounce the false resurrection of this degree,
because only Jesus Christ is the Resurrection and the Life!

In the name of Jesus Christ
I pray for the healing of...
(the stomach, gall bladder, womb, liver,
and any other organs of my body affected by Masonry),
and I ask for a release of compassion and understanding
for me and my family.

I renounce the pagan ritual of the "Point within a Circle"
with all its bondages and phallus worship.
I renounce the symbol "G" and its veiled pagan
symbolism and bondages.
I renounce the occultic mysticism of the black and white mosaic
checkered floor with the tessellated border and
five-pointed blazing star.

I renounce the All-Seeing Third Eye of Freemasonry
or Horus in the forehead and its pagan and occult symbolism.
I now close that Third Eye and all occult ability to see into the
spiritual realm, in the name of the Lord Jesus Christ,
and put my trust in the Holy Spirit sent by Jesus Christ
for all I need to know on spiritual matters.
I renounce all false communions taken,all mockery of the
redemptive work of Jesus Christ on the cross of Calvary,
all unbelief, confusion and depression.
I renounce and forsake the lie of Freemasonry
that man is not sinful,
but merely imperfect, and so can redeem himself
through good works.

I rejoice that the Bible states
that I cannot do a single thing to earn my salvation,
but that I can only be saved by grace through
faith in Jesus Christ
and what He accomplished on the
Cross of Calvary.

I renounce all fear of insanity, anguish, death wishes,
suicide and death
in the name of Jesus Christ.
Death was conquered by Jesus Christ,
and He alone holds the keys of death and hell,
and I rejoice that He holds my life in His hands now.
He came to give me life abundantly and eternally
and I believe His promises.

I renounce all anger, hatred, murderous thoughts,
revenge, retaliation, spiritual apathy, false religion, all unbelief,
especially unbelief in the Holy Bible as God's Word,
and all compromise of God's Word.
I renounce all spiritual searching into false religions,
and all striving to please God.
I rest in the knowledge that I have found my
Lord and Savior Jesus Christ,
and that He has found me.

YORK RITE

I renounce and forsake the oaths taken and the curses
involved in the York Rite Degrees of Masonry.
I renounce the Mark Lodge, and the mark in the form of

squares and angles which marks the person for life.
I also reject the jewel or occult talisman
which may have been made from this mark sign
and worn at lodge meetings;
I renounce the Mark Master Degree with its
secret word JOPPA,
and its penalty of having the right ear smote off and the
curse of permanent deafness, as well as the right hand
being chopped off for being an imposter.

I also renounce and forsake the oaths taken and the curses
involved in the other York Rite Degrees, including Past Master,
with the penalty of having my tongue split from tip to root;

and of the Most Excellent Master Degree, in which the penalty
is to have my breast torn open and my heart and vital organs
removed and exposed to rot on the dung hill.

HOLY ROYAL ARCH DEGREE

In the name of Jesus Christ,
I renounce and forsake the oaths taken and the curses
involved in the Holy Royal Arch Degree
especially the oath regarding the removal of the
head from the body
and the exposing of the brains to the hot sun.
I renounce the false secret name of God, JAHBULON,
and declare total rejection of all worship of the false pagan gods,
Bul or Baal, and On or Osiris.
I also renounce the password, AMMI RUHAMAH
and all it means.

I renounce the false communion or Eucharist
taken in this degree,
and all the mockery, skepticism and unbelief about
the redemptive work
of Jesus Christ on the cross of Calvary.
I cut off all these curses and their effects on me and my family
in the name of Jesus Christ, and I pray for...
(healing of the brain, the mind etc.).

I renounce and forsake the oaths taken and
the curses involved in the Royal Master Degree of the
York Rite; the Select Master Degree with its penalty to
have my hands chopped off to the stumps, to have my eyes
plucked out from their sockets, and to have my body quartered
and thrown among the rubbish of the Temple.

I renounce and forsake the oaths taken and the curses
involved in the Super Excellent Master Degree
along with the penalty of having my thumbs cut off,
my eyes put out, my body bound in fetters and brass,
and conveyed captive to a strange land; and also of the
Knights Order of the Red Cross,
along with the penalty of having my house
torn down and my being hanged on
the exposed timbers.

I renounce the Knights Templar Degree
and the secret words of KEB RAIOTH,
and also Knights of Malta Degree and the secret words
MAHER-SHALAL-HASH-BAZ.

I renounce the vows taken on a human skull,
the crossed swords,

and the curse and death wish of Judas of having the
head cut off and placed on top of a church spire.
I renounce the unholy communion and especially
of drinking from a human skull in many Rites.

ANCIENT AND ACCEPTED OR SCOTTISH RITE (ONLY THE 18TH, 30TH, 31ST, 32ND AND 33RD DEGREE ARE OPERATED IN BRITISH COMMONWEALTH COUNTRIES.)

*** *I renounce the oaths taken and the curses and penalties*
involved in the American and Grand Orient Lodges, including
of the Secret Master Degree, its secret password of ADONAI,
and its penalties;

*** *of the Perfect Master Degree, its secret password of MAH-*
HAH-BONE, and its penalty of being smitten to the Earth with
a setting maul;

*** *of the Intimate Secretary Degree, its secret password of*
JEHOVAH used blasphemously, and its penalties of having my
body dissected, and of having my vital organs cut into pieces
and thrown to the beasts of the field;

*** *of the Provost and Judge Degree, its secret password of*
HIRUM-TITO-CIVI-KY, and the penalty of having
my nose cut off;

*** *of the Intendant of the Building Degree,*
of its secret password
AKAR-JAI-JAH, and the penalty of having my eyes put out,
my body cut in two and exposing my bowels;

**** of the Elected Knights of the Nine Degree,*
its secret password
NEKAM NAKAH, and its penalty of having my head cut off
and stuck on the highest pole in the East;

**** of the Illustrious Elect of Fifteen Degree,*
with its secret password ELIGNAM,
and its penalties of having my body opened perpendicularly
and horizontally, the entrails exposed to the air for eight hours
so that flies may prey on them, and for my head to be cut off
and placed on a high pinnacle;

**** of the Sublime Knights elect of the Twelve Degree, its secret*
password STOLKIN-ADONAI, and its penalty of having my
hand cut in twain;

**** of the Grand Master Architect Degree, its secret password*
RAB-BANAIM, and its penalties;

**** of the Knights of the Ninth Arch of Solomon Degree,*
its secret password JEHOVAH,
and its penalty of having my body given to the
beasts of the forest as prey;

**** of the Grand Elect, Perfect and Sublime Mason Degree,*
its secret password, and its penalty of having my body cut open
and my bowels given to vultures for food;

COUNCIL OF PRINCES OF JERUSALEM

**** of the Knights of the East Degree,*
its secret password RAPH-O-DOM, and its penalties;

**** of the Prince of Jerusalem Degree,*
its secret password TEBET-ADAR
and its penalty of being stripped naked
and having my heart pierced with a ritual dagger;

CHAPTER OF THE ROSE CROIX

**** of the Knight of the East and West Degree,*
its secret password ABADDON,
and its penalty of incurring the severe wrath of the Almighty
Creator of Heaven and Earth;

18TH DEGREE

I renounce the oaths taken and the curses and penalties involved in the Eighteenth Degree of Masonry, the Most Wise Sovereign Knight of the Pelican and the Eagle and Sovereign Prince Rose Croix of Heredom.
I renounce and reject the Pelican witchcraft spirit,
as well as the occultic influence of the Rosicrucians
and the Kabbala in this degree.

I renounce the claim that the death of Jesus Christ was a "dire calamity,"
and also the deliberate mockery and twisting
of the Christian doctrine of the Atonement.
I renounce the blasphemy and rejection of the
deity of Jesus Christ, and the secret words
IGNE NATURA RENOVATUR INTEGRA
and its burning.

I renounce the mockery of the communion taken in this degree, including a biscuit, salt and white wine.

COUNCIL OF KADOSH

**** I renounce the oaths taken and the curses and penalties involved in the Grand Pontiff Degree, its secret password EMMANUEL, and its penalties;*

**** of the Grand Master of Symbolic Lodges Degree, its secret passwords JEKSON and STOLKIN, and its penalties;*

**** of the Noachite of Prussian Knight Degree, its secret password PELEG, and its penalties;*

**** of the Knight of the Royal Axe Degree, its secret password NOAH-BEZALEEL-SODONIAS, and its penalties;*

**** of the Chief of the Tabernacle Degree, its secret password URIEL-JEHOVAH, and its penalty that I agree the Earth should open up and engulf me up to my neck so I perish;*

**** of the Prince of the Tabernacle Degree, and its penalty that I should be stoned to death and my body left above ground to rot;*

**** of the Knight of the Brazen Serpent Degree, its secret password MOSES-JOHANNES, and its penalty that I have my heart eaten by venomous serpents;*

**** of the Prince of Mercy Degree,
its secret password GOMEL, JEHOVAH- JACHIN,
and its penalty of condemnation and spite
by the entire universe;*

**** of the Knight Commander of the Temple Degree,
its secret password SOLOMON,
and its penalty of receiving the severest wrath of
Almighty God inflicted upon me;*

**** of the Knight Commander of the Sun,
or Prince Adept Degree, its secret password STIBIUM,
and its penalties of having my tongue thrust through with a
red-hot iron, of my eyes being plucked out,
of my senses of smelling and hearing being removed,
of having my hands cut off and in that condition
to be left for voracious animals to devour me,
or executed by lightning from heaven;*

**** of the Grand Scottish Knight of Saint Andrew Degree,
its secret password NEKAMAH-FURLAC, and its penalties;*

**** of the Council of Kadosh Grand Pontiff Degree,
its secret password EMMANUEL, and its penalties;*

*I renounce the oaths taken and the curses involved in the
Thirtieth Degree of Masonry, the Grand Knight Kadosh and
Knight of the Black and White Eagle.
I renounce the secret passwords, STIBIUM ALKABAR, PHA-
RASH-KOH and all they mean.*

SUBLIME PRINCES OF THE ROYAL SECRET

I renounce the oaths taken and the curses
involved in the Thirty-First Degree of Masonry,
the Grand Inspector Inquisitor Commander.
I renounce all the gods and goddesses of Egypt
which are honored in this degree, including Anubis with the
ram's head, Osiris the Sun god, Isis the sister and wife of Osiris
and also the moon goddess. I renounce the Soul of Cheres,
the false symbol of immortality, the Chamber of the
dead and the false teaching of reincarnation.

I renounce the oaths taken and the curses
involved in the Thirty-Second Degree of Masonry,
the Sublime Prince of the Royal Secret.
I renounce the secret passwords,
PHAAL/PHARASH-KOL and all they mean.
I renounce Masonry's false trinitarian deity
AUM, and its parts;
Brahma the creator, Vishnu the preserver a
nd Shiva the destroyer.
I renounce the deity of AHURA-MAZDA,
the claimed spirit or source of all light,
and the worship with fire,
which is an abomination to God,
and also the drinking from a human skull in many Rites.

SHRINERS (APPLIES ONLY IN NORTH AMERICA)

*** *I renounce the oaths taken and the curses and penalties*
involved in the Ancient Arabic Order of the Nobles of the Mystic Shrine.

I renounce the piercing of the eyeballs with a three-edged blade,
the flaying of the feet, the madness,
and the worship of the false god Allah as the god of our fathers.
I renounce the hoodwink, the mock hanging, the mock beheading,
the mock drinking of the blood of the victim,
the mock dog urinating on the initiate,
and the offering of urine as a commemoration.

ALL OTHER DEGREES

I renounce all the other oaths taken,
the rituals of every other degree and the curses involved.
These include the Allied Degrees, The Red Cross of Constantine,
the Order of the Secret Monitor, and the
Masonic Royal Order of Scotland.
I renounce all other lodges and secret societies
including Prince Hall Freemasonry,
Grand Orient Lodges, Mormonism,
The Order of Amaranth, the Royal Order of Jesters,
the Manchester Unity Order of Oddfellows,
Buffalos, Druids, Foresters,
the Orange and Black Lodges, Elks, Moose and Eagles Lodges,
the Ku Klux Klan, The Grange, the Woodmen of the World,
Riders of the Red Robe, the Knights of Pythias,
the Mystic Order of the Veiled Prophets
of the Enchanted Realm,
the women's Orders of the Eastern Star,
of the Ladies Oriental Shrine,
and of the White Shrine of Jerusalem,
the girls' order of the Daughters of the Eastern Star,
the International Orders of Job's Daughters,

and of the Rainbow,
and the boys' Order of De Molay, and their effects
on me and all my family.

Lord Jesus,
because you want me to be totally free from all occult
bondages, I will burn all objects in my possession
which connect me with all lodges and occultic organizations,
including Masonry, Witchcraft and Mormonism,
and all regalia, aprons, books of rituals, rings and other jewelry.
I renounce the effects these or other objects of Masonry,
including the compass and the square,
have had on me or my family,
in the name of Jesus Christ.

I renounce every evil spirit associated with Masonry
and Witchcraft and all other sins, and I command in the
name of Jesus Christ
for Satan and every evil spirit to be bound and to leave me
now, touching or harming no one, and to go to the
place appointed for you
by the Lord Jesus, never to return to me or my family.
I call on the name of the Lord Jesus to be delivered
of these spirits,
in accordance with the many promises of the Bible.
I ask to be delivered of every spirit of sickness, infirmity, curse,
affliction, addiction, disease or allergy associated with these sins
I have confessed and renounced. I surrender to God's Holy
Spirit and to no other spirit all the places in my life
where these sins have been.

final points in the deliverance session

All participants should now be invited to sincerely carry out in faith the following actions:

1. Symbolically remove the blindfold (hoodwink) and give it to the Lord for disposal;
2. In the same way, symbolically remove the veil of mourning;
3. Symbolically cut and remove the noose from around the neck, gather it up with the cable tow running down the body and give it all to the Lord for His disposal;
4. Renounce the false Freemasonry marriage covenant, removing from the fourth finger of the right hand the ring of this false marriage covenant, giving it to the Lord to dispose of it;
5. Symbolically remove the chains and bondages of Freemasonry from your body;
6. Symbolically remove all Freemasonry regalia and armor, especially the apron;
7. Invite participants to repent of and seek forgiveness for having walked on all unholy ground, including Freemasonry lodges and temples, including any Mormon or any other occultic/Masonic organizations.
8. Symbolically remove the ball and chain from the ankles.
9. Proclaim that Satan and his demons no longer have any legal rights to mislead and manipulate the person seeking help.

concluding prayer

Holy Spirit,
I ask that you show me anything else which I need to do or to pray so that I and my family may be totally free from the consequences of the sins of Masonry, Witchcraft, Mormonism and all related Paganism and Occultism.

Pause, while listening to God, and pray as the Holy Spirit leads you.

Now, dear Father God,
I ask humbly for the blood of Jesus Christ,
your Son and my Savior,
to cleanse me from all these sins I have
confessed and renounced,
to cleanse my spirit, my soul, my mind, my emotions and every part of my body which has been affected by these sins, in the name of Jesus Christ.
I also command every cell in my body to come into divine order now, and to be healed and made whole as they were designed to be by my loving Creator, including restoring all chemical imbalances and neurological functions, controlling all cancerous cells, and reversing all degenerative diseases,
in the name of the Lord Jesus Christ.

I ask you, Lord, to baptize me in your Holy Spirit now
according to the promises in your Word.
I take to myself the whole armor of God
in accordance with Ephesians Chapter Six,
and rejoice in its protection as Jesus surrounds me and fills me with His Holy Spirit. I enthrone you, Lord Jesus, in my heart,

for you are my Lord and my Savior, the source of eternal life. Thank you, Father God, for your mercy, your forgiveness and your love, in the name of Jesus Christ, amen.

Since the above is what needs to be renounced, why would anyone want to join? Copying of this prayer is both permitted and encouraged, provided reference is made to where it comes from. Written testimonies of changed lives and healings are welcome. Additions to this prayer will be added to our Internet site (address below) as well as for other lodges or secret or occultic organizations. These may be freely downloaded for wider use. If additional prayer and ministry are required following the above prayer, please contact the Jubilee Essential Resources, who may refer you to someone closer to you. We have competent counselors in most countries around the world.

For further information please contact:
Jubilee Ministries Trust, Incorporated
P. O. Box 36-044
Wellington 6330
New Zealand
Phone/Fax 64-4-568-4533
Website: www.jubilee.org.nz

Index

O

P

Q

R

S

T